Quick & Easy
Dump
Cakes
AND MORE

Publications International, Ltd.

Louis Weber, CEO
Publications International, Ltd.
7373 North Cicero Avenue
Lincolnwood, IL 60712

TELEBrands PRESS

Telebrands Press
79 Two Bridges Road
Fairfield, NJ 07004
www.telebrands.com

Pictured on the front cover: Cherry Cheesecake Dump Cake *(page 19)*.

Pictured on the back cover (from top): Mixed Berry Cake *(page 37)*, Island Delight Cake *(page 83)* and Simple S'More Cake *(page 63)*.

Library of Congress Control Number: 2013949291

ISBN: 978-0-9895865-2-8

Manufactured in U.S.A.

8 7

Microwave Cooking: Microwave ovens vary in wattage. Use the cooking times as guidelines and check for doneness before adding more time.

About Cathy: Cathy Mitchell has been cooking for 60 years, starting at her grandmother's side, standing on a stool. She never refers to herself as a chef, but rather a great home cook who enjoys making simple, easy meals with ordinary ingredients. She has been sharing those ideas on television since her first commercial in 1989, introducing America to the electric sandwich maker, and in typical Cathy fashion, making a lot more than sandwiches.

Cathy has an extended family of five adult kids, ranging in age from 31 to 43, and ten grandkids from 1 to 20. One of her favorite stories is overhearing her oldest son's response when a dinner guest commented before dinner that he didn't really like something on the menu. He said, "Well, maybe not before, but you haven't tried my Mom's yet!"

Publications International, Ltd.

TABLE
of Contents

CLASSIC
Dump Cakes

Apple Peach Cake

- 2 cans (21 ounces each) apple pie filling
- 2 cans (15 ounces each) peach slices, drained
- 1 teaspoon ground cinnamon, divided
- ½ teaspoon ground nutmeg, divided
- 1 package (about 15 ounces) white cake mix
- ½ cup (1 stick) butter, melted

1. Preheat oven to 350°F. Spray 13×9-inch baking pan with nonstick cooking spray.

2. Spread apple pie filling and peaches in prepared pan. Sprinkle with ½ teaspoon cinnamon and ¼ teaspoon nutmeg. Top with cake mix, spreading evenly. Pour butter over top, covering cake mix as much as possible. Sprinkle with remaining ½ teaspoon cinnamon and ¼ teaspoon nutmeg.

3. Bake 1 hour or until top is lightly browned and toothpick inserted into center of cake comes out clean. Cool at least 15 minutes before serving.

Makes 12 to 16 servings

Banana Split Cake

Pictured on page 145

- **1 can (20 ounces) crushed pineapple, undrained**
- **1 can (15 ounces) tart cherries in water, drained**
- **1 package (about 18 ounces) banana cake mix**
- **½ cup (1 stick) butter, cut into thin slices**
- **½ cup semisweet chocolate chips**
- **½ cup chopped pecans**
- **Whipped cream and maraschino cherries (optional)**

1. Preheat oven to 350°F. Spray 13×9-inch baking pan with nonstick cooking spray.

2. Spread pineapple and cherries in prepared pan. Top with cake mix, spreading evenly. Top with butter in single layer, covering cake mix as much as possible. Sprinkle with chocolate chips and pecans.

3. Bake 55 to 60 minutes or until toothpick inserted into center of cake comes out clean. Cool at least 15 minutes before serving. Top with whipped cream and cherries, if desired. *Makes 12 to 16 servings*

Cherry Vanilla Cake

1 package (about 15 ounces) vanilla cake mix

3 eggs

½ cup vegetable or canola oil

1 can (21 ounces) cherry pie filling

1. Preheat oven to 350°F. Spray 13×9-inch baking pan with nonstick cooking spray.

2. Combine cake mix, eggs and oil in large bowl; beat 1 to 2 minutes or until well blended. Fold in cherry pie filling. Spread batter in prepared pan.

3. Bake 25 to 30 minutes or until toothpick inserted into center comes out clean. Cool completely in pan on wire rack.   *Makes 12 to 16 servings*

Blueberry Cinnamon Cake

2 packages (12 ounces each) frozen blueberries, thawed and drained

⅓ cup sugar

¾ teaspoon ground cinnamon, divided

1 package (about 15 ounces) yellow cake mix

¾ cup (1½ sticks) butter, cut into thin slices

1. Preheat oven to 350°F. Spray 13×9-inch baking pan with nonstick cooking spray.

2. Spread blueberries in prepared pan. Sprinkle with sugar and ½ teaspoon cinnamon; toss to coat. Top with cake mix, spreading evenly. Top with butter in single layer, covering cake mix as much as possible. Sprinkle with remaining ¼ teaspoon cinnamon.

3. Bake 50 to 60 minutes or until toothpick inserted into center of cake comes out clean. Cool at least 15 minutes before serving.

Makes 12 to 16 servings

Apple Pie Dump Cake

1 can (21 ounces) apple pie filling

1 package (about 15 ounces) white cake mix

3 eggs

½ cup vegetable or canola oil

⅓ cup chopped pecans

1. Preheat oven to 350°F. Spray 13×9-inch baking pan with nonstick cooking spray.

2. Place apple pie filling in large bowl; cut apple slices into chunks with paring knife or scissors. Add cake mix, eggs and oil; beat 1 to 2 minutes or until well blended. Spread batter in prepared pan; sprinkle with pecans.

3. Bake 40 to 45 minutes or until toothpick inserted into center comes out clean. Cool in pan at least 15 minutes before serving.

Makes 12 to 16 servings

Peach Melba Cake

Pictured on page 146

- **2 cans (21 ounces each) peach pie filling**
- **1 package (12 ounces) frozen raspberries, thawed and drained**
- **1 package (about 15 ounces) yellow cake mix**
- **½ cup (1 stick) butter, cut into thin slices**

1. Preheat oven to 350°F. Spray 13×9-inch baking pan with nonstick cooking spray.

2. Spread peach pie filling in prepared pan; sprinkle with raspberries. Top with cake mix, spreading evenly. Top with butter in single layer, covering cake mix as much as possible.

3. Bake 40 to 45 minutes or until toothpick inserted into center of cake comes out clean. Cool at least 15 minutes before serving.

Makes 12 to 16 servings

Carrot Banana Cake

1 package (about 15 ounces) carrot cake mix, plus ingredients to prepare mix

1 teaspoon baking soda

2 bananas, mashed (about 1 heaping cup)

1 cup chopped walnuts

½ cup raisins

Prepared cream cheese frosting, warmed (optional)

Additional chopped walnuts (optional)

1. Preheat oven to 350°F. Grease and flour 12-cup (10-inch) bundt pan.

2. Prepare cake mix according to package directions. Stir baking soda into mashed bananas; add to batter and beat until well blended. Stir in 1 cup walnuts and raisins. Pour batter into prepared pan.

3. Bake 40 to 45 minutes or until toothpick inserted near center comes out clean. Cool in pan 10 minutes; invert onto wire rack to cool completely. Drizzle with cream cheese frosting and sprinkle with additional walnuts, if desired.

Makes 12 servings

Cha-Cha-Cha Cherry Cake

2 packages (12 ounces each) frozen cherries, thawed and drained

1 package (4-serving size) cherry gelatin

1 package (about 15 ounces) white cake mix

½ cup (1 stick) butter, cut into thin slices

1 cup chopped walnuts

¼ cup water

1. Preheat oven to 350°F. Spray 9-inch square baking pan with nonstick cooking spray.

2. Spread cherries in prepared pan; sprinkle with gelatin. Top with cake mix, spreading evenly. Top with butter in single layer, covering cake mix as much as possible. Sprinkle with walnuts. Drizzle water over top.

3. Bake 50 to 60 minutes or until toothpick inserted into center of cake comes out clean. Cool at least 15 minutes before serving.   *Makes 9 servings*

Blueberry Peach Almond Cake

　　1　can (29 ounces) peach slices in light syrup, undrained
　　1　can (21 ounces) blueberry pie filling
　　1　package (about 15 ounces) yellow cake mix
　　½　cup (1 stick) butter, cut into thin slices
　　1　cup sliced almonds

1. Preheat oven to 350°F. Spray 13×9-inch baking pan with nonstick cooking spray.

2. Drain peaches, reserving syrup. Spread peaches in prepared pan; cut into chunks with paring knife or scissors. Add blueberry pie filling and ½ cup reserved syrup to pan. Top with cake mix, spreading evenly. Top with butter in single layer, covering cake mix as much as possible. Sprinkle with almonds.

3. Bake 45 to 50 minutes or until toothpick inserted into center of cake comes out clean. Cool at least 15 minutes before serving.

Makes 12 to 16 servings

Banana Strawberry Cake

1 can (21 ounces) strawberry pie filling

1 can (20 ounces) crushed pineapple, undrained

1 package (about 18 ounces) banana cake mix

½ cup (1 stick) butter, cut into thin slices

1. Preheat oven to 350°F. Spray 13×9-inch baking pan with nonstick cooking spray.

2. Spread strawberry pie filling and pineapple in prepared pan. Top with cake mix, spreading evenly. Top with butter in single layer, covering as much cake mix as possible.

3. Bake 45 to 50 minutes or until toothpick inserted into center of cake comes out clean. Cool at least 15 minutes before serving.

Makes 12 to 16 servings

Classic Apple Dump Cake

- 1 can (21 ounces) apple pie filling
- 1 package (9 ounces) yellow cake mix
- ¼ cup (½ stick) butter, cut into thin slices
- ¼ teaspoon ground cinnamon
- ⅛ teaspoon ground ginger
- ½ cup chopped walnuts

1. Preheat oven to 350°F. Spray 9-inch square baking pan with nonstick cooking spray.

2. Spread apple pie filling in prepared pan. Top with cake mix, spreading evenly. Top with butter in single layer, covering cake mix as much as possible. Sprinkle with cinnamon, ginger and walnuts.

3. Bake 35 to 40 minutes or until toothpick inserted into center of cake comes out clean. Cool at least 15 minutes before serving. *Makes 9 servings*

Red, White & Blue Cake

- 1 can (21 ounces) cherry pie filling
- 1 package (12 ounces) frozen blueberries, thawed and drained
  or 2½ cups fresh blueberries
- ¼ teaspoon ground cinnamon
- 1 package (about 15 ounces) white cake mix
- ¾ cup (1½ sticks) butter, cut into thin slices

1. Preheat oven to 350°F. Spray 13×9-inch baking pan with nonstick cooking spray.

2. Spread cherry pie filling and blueberries in prepared pan; sprinkle with cinnamon. Top with cake mix, spreading evenly. Top with butter in single layer, covering cake mix as much as possible.

3. Bake 45 to 50 minutes or until toothpick inserted into center of cake comes out clean. Cool at least 15 minutes before serving.

Makes 12 to 16 servings

Peach Crunch Cake

1 can (29 ounces) peach slices in light syrup, undrained
1 package (about 15 ounces) yellow cake mix
¼ teaspoon ground cinnamon
½ cup (1 stick) butter, cut into thin slices
½ cup packed brown sugar
1 cup pecan halves

1. Preheat oven to 350°F. Spray 13×9-inch baking pan with nonstick cooking spray.

2. Spread peaches in prepared pan. Top with cake mix, spreading evenly. Sprinkle with cinnamon. Top with butter in single layer, covering cake mix as much as possible. Sprinkle with brown sugar and pecans.

3. Bake 40 to 50 minutes or until toothpick inserted into center of cake comes out clean. Cool at least 15 minutes before serving.

Makes 12 to 16 servings

Lemon Poppy Seed Cake

- 1 package (about 15 ounces) yellow cake mix
- 1 package (4-serving size) lemon gelatin
- 4 eggs
- ⅔ cup water
- ½ cup vegetable or canola oil
  Grated peel and juice of ½ lemon
- ¼ cup poppy seeds
  Lemon Glaze (optional, recipe follows)

1. Preheat oven to 350°F. Grease and flour 12-cup (10-inch) bundt pan.

2. Combine cake mix, gelatin, eggs, water, oil, lemon peel and juice in large bowl; beat 1 to 2 minutes or until well blended. Stir in poppy seeds. Pour batter into prepared pan.

3. Bake about 35 minutes or until toothpick inserted near center comes out clean. Cool in pan 10 minutes; invert onto wire rack to cool completely.

4. Prepare Lemon Glaze, if desired. Drizzle over cooled cake.

Makes 12 servings

Lemon Glaze: Whisk 1 cup powdered sugar and 2 tablespoons lemon juice in small bowl until smooth.

Strawberry Marshmallow Cake

1 package (about 15 ounces) vanilla cake mix, plus ingredients to prepare mix

⅓ cup mini semisweet chocolate chips

2 cups sliced fresh or thawed frozen strawberries

1 package (4-serving size) strawberry gelatin

¼ cup water

2½ cups mini marshmallows

1. Preheat oven to 350°F. Spray 9-inch square baking pan with nonstick cooking spray.

2. Prepare cake mix according to package directions; stir in chocolate chips. Spread strawberries in prepared pan. Sprinkle with gelatin; drizzle water over top. Sprinkle with marshmallows; spread batter evenly over marshmallows.

3. Bake 40 to 45 minutes or until toothpick inserted into center of cake comes out clean. Cool at least 15 minutes before serving.   *Makes 9 servings*

FAMILY
Favorites

Cherry Cheesecake Dump Cake

Pictured on page 147

- 1 can (21 ounces) cherry pie filling
- 1 can (14½ ounces) tart cherries in water, drained
- 4 ounces cream cheese, cut into small pieces
- 1 package (about 15 ounces) yellow cake mix
- ½ cup (1 stick) butter, cut into thin slices

1. Preheat oven to 350°F. Spray 13×9-inch baking pan with nonstick cooking spray.

2. Spread cherry pie filling and cherries in prepared pan. Scatter cream cheese pieces over cherries. Top with cake mix, spreading evenly. Top with butter in single layer, covering cake mix as much as possible.

3. Bake 45 to 50 minutes or until toothpick inserted into center of cake comes out clean. Cool at least 15 minutes before serving.

Makes 12 to 16 servings

Double Banana Cake

1 package (about 18 ounces) banana cake mix, plus ingredients to prepare mix
¾ cup chopped hazelnuts or sliced almonds, toasted,* divided
1 banana, thinly sliced
¼ cup chocolate hazelnut spread, warmed**

To toast hazelnuts, spread in single layer on baking sheet. Bake at 350°F 7 to 10 minutes or until golden brown, stirring occasionally. Remove hazelnuts from pan and cool completely before chopping.

**Microwave spread on LOW (30%) about 1 minute or until pourable.*

1. Preheat oven to 350°F. Spray 9-inch square baking pan with nonstick cooking spray.

2. Prepare cake mix according to package directions; stir in ½ cup hazelnuts. Spread half of batter in prepared pan. Top with banana slices; drizzle with 2 tablespoons chocolate hazelnut spread. Top with remaining half of batter; sprinkle with remaining ¼ cup hazelnuts and drizzle with 2 tablespoons chocolate hazelnut spread.

3. Bake 25 to 30 minutes or until toothpick inserted into center comes out clean. Cool in pan at least 15 minutes before serving.   *Makes 9 servings*

Honey of a Peach Cake

  1 **can (21 ounces) peach pie filling**
  1 **package (about 15 ounces) yellow cake mix**
  ½ **cup (1 stick) butter, cut into thin slices**
  2 **tablespoons honey**
  ½ **cup chopped honey-roasted almonds**

1. Preheat oven to 350°F. Spray 9-inch square baking pan with nonstick cooking spray.

2. Spread peach pie filling in prepared pan. Top with cake mix, spreading evenly. Top with butter in single layer, covering cake mix as much as possible. Drizzle with honey; sprinkle with almonds.

3. Bake 50 to 60 minutes or until toothpick inserted into center of cake comes out clean. Cool at least 15 minutes before serving.   *Makes 9 servings*

Pink Lemonade Cake

3 cups fresh or thawed frozen sliced strawberries

¼ cup powdered pink lemonade mix

1 package (about 15 ounces) white cake mix

½ cup (1 stick) butter, cut into thin slices

½ cup water

1. Preheat oven to 350°F. Spray 9-inch square baking pan with nonstick cooking spray.

2. Spread strawberries in prepared pan; sprinkle with lemonade mix. Top with cake mix, spreading evenly. Top with butter in single layer. Slowly pour water over top, covering cake mix as much as possible.

3. Bake 40 to 45 minutes or until toothpick inserted into center of cake comes out clean. Cool at least 15 minutes before serving.   *Makes 9 servings*

Sweet-Hot Apple Dump Cake

 2 cans (21 ounces each) apple pie filling

 ¼ cup plus 2 tablespoons hot cinnamon candies, divided

 1 package (about 15 ounces) yellow cake mix

 ½ cup (1 stick) butter, cut into thin slices

1. Preheat oven to 350°F. Spray 13×9-inch baking pan with nonstick cooking spray.

2. Spread apple pie filling in prepared pan. Sprinkle with ¼ cup cinnamon candies. Top with cake mix, spreading evenly. Top with butter in single layer, covering cake mix as much as possible.

3. Bake 45 to 55 minutes or until toothpick inserted into center of cake comes out clean, sprinkling with remaining 2 tablespoons cinnamon candies during last 10 minutes of baking. Cool at least 15 minutes before serving.

Makes 12 to 16 servings

Caramel Candy Cake

1 package (about 15 ounces) yellow cake mix

2 eggs

½ cup (1 stick) butter, melted

½ cup milk

1 package (8 ounces) unwrapped bite-size chocolate peanut caramel candies, chopped, divided

2 tablespoons caramel topping, warmed

1. Preheat oven to 350°F. Spray 9-inch square baking pan with nonstick cooking spray.

2. Combine cake mix, eggs, butter and milk in large bowl; beat 1 to 2 minutes or until well blended. Stir in half of candy. Spread batter in prepared pan; sprinkle with remaining candy. Drizzle with caramel topping.

3. Bake 30 to 35 minutes or until toothpick inserted into center comes out clean. Cool in pan at least 15 minutes before serving.   *Makes 9 servings*

Peachy Keen Cake

1 can (29 ounces) peach slices in light syrup, undrained
Water
1 package (4-serving size) peach gelatin
1 package (about 15 ounces) yellow cake mix
½ cup (1 stick) butter, cut into thin slices

1. Preheat oven to 350°F. Spray 9-inch square baking pan with nonstick cooking spray.

2. Drain peaches, reserving liquid in measuring cup. Add water to equal 1 cup.

3. Spread peaches in prepared pan; cut into chunks with paring knife or scissors. Sprinkle with gelatin. Top with cake mix, spreading evenly. Top with butter in single layer. Slowly pour peach liquid over top, covering cake mix as much as possible.

4. Bake 55 to 60 minutes or until toothpick inserted into center of cake comes out clean. Cool at least 15 minutes before serving.   *Makes 9 servings*

Best Banana Cake

1 **package (about 15 ounces) vanilla cake mix, plus ingredients to prepare mix**
2 **bananas, mashed (about 1 heaping cup)**
1 **teaspoon baking soda**

1. Preheat oven to 350°F. Spray 13×9-inch baking pan with nonstick cooking spray.

2. Prepare cake mix according to package directions. Stir baking soda into bananas; add to batter and beat until well blended. Spread batter in prepared pan.

3. Bake 35 to 40 minutes or until toothpick inserted into center comes out almost clean. Cool completely in pan on wire rack.

Makes 12 to 16 servings

Cherry Orange Cake

 1 can (15 ounces) mandarin oranges in light syrup, undrained
 1 package (12 ounces) frozen cherries, thawed and drained
 1 package (about 15 ounces) yellow cake mix
 ½ cup flaked coconut
 ½ cup sliced almonds
 ½ cup (1 stick) butter, melted

1. Preheat oven to 350°F. Spray 9-inch square baking pan with nonstick cooking spray.

2. Spread mandarin oranges and cherries in prepared pan. Top with cake mix, spreading evenly. Sprinkle with coconut and almonds. Pour butter over top, covering cake mix as much as possible.

3. Bake 35 to 40 minutes or until toothpick inserted into center of cake comes out clean. (If desired, turn oven to broil and broil cake 1 minute to brown top of cake.) Cool at least 15 minutes before serving.

Makes 9 servings

Super Fruity Confetti Cake

2 cans (15 ounces each) fruit cocktail, drained

1 package (about 15 ounces) white cake mix

½ cup (1 stick) butter, cut into thin slices

¼ cup multicolored tiny crunchy tangy candies

1. Preheat oven to 350°F. Spray 13×9-inch baking pan with nonstick cooking spray.

2. Spread fruit cocktail in prepared pan. Top with cake mix, spreading evenly. Top with butter in single layer, covering cake mix as much as possible.

3. Bake 45 to 50 minutes or until toothpick inserted into center of cake comes out clean, sprinkling with candies during last 20 minutes of baking. Cool at least 15 minutes before serving. *Makes 12 to 16 servings*

Lemon Cream Cheese Cake

1 can (about 16 ounces) lemon pie filling

1 package (about 15 ounces) yellow cake mix

4 ounces cream cheese, cut into small pieces

½ cup (1 stick) butter, cut into thin slices

1. Preheat oven to 350°F. Spray 9-inch square baking pan with nonstick cooking spray.

2. Spread lemon pie filling in prepared pan. Top with half of cake mix; dot with cream cheese and cover with remaining cake mix. Top with butter in single layer, covering cake mix as much as possible.

3. Bake 35 to 40 minutes or until toothpick inserted into center of cake comes out clean. Cool at least 15 minutes before serving.   *Makes 9 servings*

Salted Caramel Banana Cake

3 bananas, mashed (about 1½ cups)

1 teaspoon coarse salt

¼ cup caramel topping, warmed, divided

1 package (about 18 ounces) banana cake mix

½ cup (1 stick) butter, cut into thin slices

1. Preheat oven to 350°F. Spray 13×9-inch baking pan with nonstick cooking spray.

2. Spread mashed bananas in prepared pan. Stir salt into caramel; drizzle half of mixture over bananas. Top with cake mix, spreading evenly. Top with butter in single layer, covering cake mix as much as possible. Drizzle with remaining caramel mixture.

3. Bake 30 to 35 minutes or until toothpick inserted into center of cake comes out clean. Cool at least 15 minutes before serving.

Makes 12 to 16 servings

Cinnamon Chip Pumpkin Cake

- 1 package (about 15 ounces) yellow cake mix
- 1 can (15 ounces) solid-pack pumpkin
- 2 eggs
- ½ cup water
- 2 teaspoons pumpkin pie spice
- ½ cup cinnamon chips, divided
- ½ cup chopped pecans, divided

1. Preheat oven to 350°F. Spray 13×9-inch baking pan with nonstick cooking spray.

2. Combine cake mix, pumpkin, eggs, water and pumpkin pie spice in large bowl; beat 1 to 2 minutes or until well blended. Stir in ¼ cup cinnamon chips and ¼ cup pecans. Spread batter in prepared pan; sprinkle with remaining cinnamon chips and pecans.

3. Bake 25 to 30 minutes or until toothpick inserted into center comes out clean. Cool in pan at least 15 minutes before serving.

Makes 12 to 16 servings

Apple Toffee Cake

   1 can (21 ounces) apple pie filling
   1 package (about 15 ounces) yellow cake mix
   ½ cup (1 stick) butter, cut into thin slices
   ⅓ cup toffee bits

1. Preheat oven to 350°F. Spray 8- or 9-inch square baking pan with nonstick cooking spray.

2. Spread apple pie filling in prepared pan. Top with cake mix, spreading evenly. Top with butter in single layer, covering cake mix as much as possible. Sprinkle with toffee bits.

3. Bake 50 to 60 minutes or until toothpick inserted into center of cake comes out clean. Cool at least 15 minutes before serving.   *Makes 9 servings*

Almond Peach Cake

　2　cans (29 ounces each) peach slices in light syrup, undrained
　½　teaspoon almond extract
　1　package (about 15 ounces) white cake mix
　½　cup (1 stick) butter, cut into thin slices
　1　cup crumbled Chinese-style almond cookies or almond biscotti

1. Preheat oven to 350°F. Spray 13×9-inch baking pan with nonstick cooking spray.

2. Drain peaches, reserving 1 cup syrup. Cut peaches into ½-inch chunks with paring knife or scissors. Combine peaches, reserved syrup and almond extract in prepared pan. Top with cake mix, spreading evenly. Top with butter in single layer, covering cake mix as much as possible. Sprinkle with crumbled cookies.

3. Bake 50 to 55 minutes or until toothpick inserted into center of cake comes out clean. Cool at least 15 minutes before serving.

Makes 12 to 16 servings

Rainbow Cake

Pictured on page 148

   1 **can (20 ounces) crushed pineapple, undrained**

   1 **can (14½ ounces) tart cherries in water, drained**

   1 **package (about 15 ounces) yellow cake mix**

   ½ **cup (1 stick) butter, cut into thin slices**

   ½ **cup candy-coated chocolate pieces**

1. Preheat oven to 350°F. Spray 13×9-inch baking pan with nonstick cooking spray.

2. Spread pineapple and cherries in prepared pan. Top with cake mix, spreading evenly. Top with butter in single layer, covering cake mix as much as possible.

3. Bake 35 to 40 minutes or until toothpick inserted into center of cake comes out clean, sprinkling with chocolate pieces during last 10 minutes of baking. Cool at least 15 minutes before serving.   *Makes 12 to 16 servings*

VERY
Berry

Double Strawberry Cake

  3 cups fresh or thawed frozen sliced strawberries

  1 package (4-serving size) strawberry gelatin

  1 package (about 15 ounces) yellow cake mix

  ½ cup (1 stick) butter, cut into thin slices

  ⅓ cup water

1. Preheat oven to 350°F. Spray 9-inch square baking pan with nonstick cooking spray.

2. Spread strawberries in prepared pan; sprinkle with gelatin. Top with cake mix, spreading evenly. Top with butter in single layer, covering cake mix as much as possible. Drizzle water over top.

3. Bake 45 to 50 minutes or until toothpick inserted into center of cake comes out clean. Cool at least 15 minutes before serving. *Makes 9 servings*

Raspberry Yogurt Cake

1 can (21 ounces) raspberry pie filling
1 cup Greek yogurt
1 cup water
1 package (about 15 ounces) yellow cake mix
Grated peel of 1 lemon

1. Preheat oven to 350°F. Spray 13×9-inch baking pan with nonstick cooking spray.

2. Spread raspberry pie filling in prepared pan. Whisk yogurt and water in large bowl until blended. Add cake mix and lemon peel; beat 1 to 2 minutes or until well blended. Spread batter evenly over raspberry filling.

3. Bake 30 to 35 minutes or until toothpick inserted into center of cake comes out clean. Cool at least 15 minutes before serving.

Makes 12 to 16 servings

Mixed Berry Cake

Pictured on page 149

> **2** packages (12 ounces each) frozen mixed berries, thawed and drained
>
> **1** package (about 15 ounces) white cake mix
>
> **¼** teaspoon ground cinnamon
>
> **1** can (12 ounces) lemon-lime soda
>
> **½** cup cinnamon chips

1. Preheat oven to 350°F. Spray 13×9-inch baking pan with nonstick cooking spray.

2. Spread mixed berries in prepared pan. Top with cake mix, spreading evenly. Sprinkle with cinnamon. Slowly pour soda over top, covering cake mix as much as possible. Sprinkle with cinnamon chips.

3. Bake 45 to 50 minutes or until toothpick inserted into center of cake comes out clean. Cool at least 15 minutes before serving.

Makes 12 to 16 servings

Blueberry Lemon Dump Cake

- 1 can (21 ounces) blueberry pie filling
- 1 can (20 ounces) crushed pineapple, undrained
- 1 package (about 18 ounces) lemon cake mix
- ½ cup (1 stick) butter, cut into thin slices

1. Preheat oven to 350°F. Spray 13×9-inch baking pan with nonstick cooking spray.

2. Spread blueberry pie filling and pineapple in prepared pan. Top with cake mix, spreading evenly. Top with butter in single layer, covering cake mix as much as possible.

3. Bake 50 to 55 minutes or until toothpick inserted into center of cake comes out clean. Cool at least 15 minutes before serving.

Makes 12 to 16 servings

Peach Strawberry Cake

    1   can (29 ounces) peach slices in light syrup, undrained
1½   cups frozen sliced strawberries, thawed and drained
    1   package (about 15 ounces) yellow cake mix
  ½   cup (1 stick) butter, melted

1. Preheat oven to 350°F. Spray 13×9-inch baking pan with nonstick cooking spray.

2. Spread peaches and strawberries in prepared pan. Top with cake mix, spreading evenly. Pour butter over top, covering cake mix as much as possible.

3. Bake 50 to 55 minutes or until toothpick inserted into center of cake comes out clean. Cool at least 15 minutes before serving.

Makes 12 to 16 servings

Cranberry Lemon Cake

- 1 can (20 ounces) crushed pineapple, undrained
- 1 can (14 ounces) whole berry cranberry sauce
- 1 package (about 18 ounces) lemon cake mix
- ¾ cup (1½ sticks) butter, melted

1. Preheat oven to 350°F. Spray 13×9-inch baking pan with nonstick cooking spray.

2. Spread pineapple and cranberry sauce in prepared pan. Top with cake mix, spreading evenly. Pour butter over top, covering cake mix as much as possible.

3. Bake 50 to 55 minutes or until toothpick inserted into center of cake comes out clean. Cool at least 15 minutes before serving.

Makes 12 to 16 servings

Berry Cobbler Cake

2 cups (1 pint) fresh or frozen berries (blueberries, blackberries and/or raspberries)

1 package (9 ounces) yellow cake mix

1 teaspoon ground cinnamon

1 egg

1 cup water, divided

¼ cup sugar

1 tablespoon cornstarch

1. Preheat oven to 375°F. Spray 9-inch square baking pan with nonstick cooking spray.

2. Spread berries in prepared pan. Combine cake mix and cinnamon in large bowl. Add egg and ¼ cup water; stir until well blended. Spread batter over berries.

3. Combine sugar and cornstarch in same bowl. Stir in remaining ¾ cup water until sugar mixture dissolves; pour over cake batter. Do not stir.

4. Bake 40 to 45 minutes or until lightly browned. Cool at least 15 minutes before serving. Serve warm or at room temperature. *Makes 6 servings*

Super Strawberry Dump Cake

3 cups thawed frozen or fresh strawberries, cut into halves or quarters

1 package (about 15 ounces) strawberry cake mix

½ cup (1 stick) butter, cut into thin slices

1. Preheat oven to 350°F. Spray 13×9-inch baking pan with nonstick cooking spray.

2. Spread strawberries in prepared pan. Top with cake mix, spreading evenly. Top with butter in single layer, covering cake mix as much as possible.

3. Bake 45 to 50 minutes or until toothpick inserted into center of cake comes out clean. Cool at least 15 minutes before serving.

Makes 12 to 16 servings

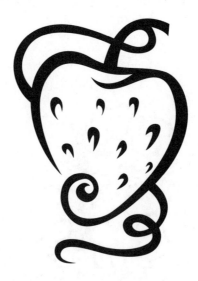

Blackberry Almond Cake

Pictured on page 150

- 2 packages (12 ounces each) frozen blackberries, thawed and drained
- ¼ cup granulated sugar
- 1 package (about 15 ounces) yellow cake mix
- ¾ cup (1½ sticks) butter, cut into thin slices
- ½ cup sliced almonds
- ¼ cup packed brown sugar

1. Preheat oven to 350°F. Spray 13×9-inch baking pan with nonstick cooking spray.

2. Spread blackberries in prepared pan; sprinkle with granulated sugar and toss to coat. Top with cake mix, spreading evenly. Top with butter in single layer, covering cake mix as much as possible. Sprinkle with almonds and brown sugar.

3. Bake 50 to 60 minutes or until toothpick inserted into center of cake comes out clean. Cool at least 15 minutes before serving.

Makes 12 to 16 servings

Raspberry Lovers' Cake

Pictured on page 151

- **1 can (21 ounces) raspberry pie filling**
- **1 package (12 ounces) frozen raspberries, thawed and drained**
- **1 package (12 ounces) semisweet chocolate chips, divided**
- **1 package (about 15 ounces) white cake mix**
- **¾ cup (1½ sticks) butter, cut into thin slices**
- **½ cup packed brown sugar**

1. Preheat oven to 350°F. Spray 13×9-inch baking pan with nonstick cooking spray.

2. Spread raspberry pie filling in prepared pan; sprinkle with raspberries. Sprinkle with half of chocolate chips. Top with cake mix, spreading evenly. Top with butter in single layer, covering cake mix as much as possible. Sprinkle with brown sugar and remaining chocolate chips.

3. Bake 45 to 50 minutes or until toothpick inserted into center of cake comes out clean. Cool at least 15 minutes before serving.

Makes 12 to 16 servings

Peach Cranberry Upside Down Cake

¼ cup (½ stick) butter, melted

½ cup packed brown sugar

3 cups thawed frozen or canned peach slices (thick slices cut in half)

2 cups fresh or thawed frozen cranberries

1 package (about 15 ounces) yellow cake mix, plus ingredients to prepare mix

1. Preheat oven to 350°F. Spray two 9-inch round cake pans with nonstick cooking spray.

2. Divide butter and brown sugar between prepared pans; spread evenly over bottoms of pans. Arrange peach slices over butter mixture; sprinkle with cranberries.

3. Prepare cake mix according to package directions. Spread batter over fruit in each pan.

4. Bake 30 to 35 minutes or until toothpick inserted into center of cakes comes out clean. Cool 5 minutes; invert cakes onto serving plates. Serve warm or at room temperature. *Makes 12 to 16 servings*

Blueberry Vanilla Cake

  2 packages (12 ounces each) frozen blueberries, thawed and drained
      or 5 cups fresh blueberries

  6 tablespoons sugar, divided

  ¾ teaspoon ground cinnamon, divided

  1 package (about 15 ounces) vanilla cake mix

  ¾ cup (1½ sticks) butter, cut into thin slices

1. Preheat oven to 350°F. Spray two 9-inch pie plates with nonstick cooking spray.*

2. Spread one package of blueberries in each prepared pie plate. Sprinkle each with 2 tablespoons sugar and ¼ teaspoon cinnamon. Top with cake mix, spreading evenly. Top with butter in single layer, covering cake mix as much as possible. Sprinkle with remaining 2 tablespoons sugar and ¼ teaspoon cinnamon.

3. Bake 50 to 55 minutes or until toothpick inserted into center of cakes comes out clean. Cool at least 15 minutes before serving.

Makes 12 to 16 servings

*Or use one 13×9-inch baking pan instead of two pie plates.

Very Berry Cheesecake Dump Cake

1 can (21 ounces) strawberry pie filling

1 package (12 ounces) frozen blackberries, thawed and drained

4 ounces cream cheese, cut into small pieces

1 package (about 15 ounces) yellow cake mix

½ cup (1 stick) butter, cut into thin slices

1. Preheat oven to 350°F. Spray 13×9-inch baking pan with nonstick cooking spray.

2. Spread strawberry pie filling and blackberries in prepared pan. Scatter cream cheese pieces over fruit. Top with cake mix, spreading evenly. Top with butter in single layer, covering cake mix as much as possible.

3. Bake 45 to 50 minutes or until toothpick inserted into center of cake comes out clean. Cool at least 15 minutes before serving.

Makes 12 to 16 servings

Raspberry Lemon Cake

2 packages (12 ounces each) frozen raspberries, thawed and drained

⅔ cup sugar

Grated peel of 1 lemon

1 package (about 18 ounces) lemon cake mix

¾ cup (1½ sticks) butter, cut into thin slices

1. Preheat oven to 350°F. Spray 13×9-inch baking pan with nonstick cooking spray.

2. Spread raspberries in prepared pan. Sprinkle with sugar; toss to coat. Sprinkle with lemon peel. Top with cake mix, spreading evenly. Top with butter in single layer, covering cake mix as much as possible.

3. Bake 50 to 55 minutes or until toothpick inserted into center of cake comes out clean. Cool at least 15 minutes before serving.

Makes 12 to 16 servings

Blackberry Bonanza Dump Cake

  2 **packages (12 ounces each) frozen blackberries, thawed and drained**

  1 **package (4-serving size) blackberry gelatin**

  1 **package (about 15 ounces) white cake mix**

 ½ **cup (1 stick) butter, cut into thin slices**

  1 **cup chopped pecans**

 ¼ **cup water**

1. Preheat oven to 350°F. Spray 9-inch square baking pan with nonstick cooking spray.

2. Spread blackberries in prepared pan; sprinkle with gelatin. Top with cake mix, spreading evenly. Top with butter in single layer, covering cake mix as much as possible. Sprinkle with pecans. Drizzle water over top.

3. Bake 50 to 55 minutes or until toothpick inserted into center of cake comes out clean. Cool at least 15 minutes before serving.   *Makes 9 servings*

Strawberry Banana Cake

1 package (about 15 ounces) strawberry cake mix, plus ingredients to prepare mix

1 teaspoon baking soda

2 bananas, mashed (about 1 heaping cup)

1. Preheat oven to 350°F. Spray 13×9-inch baking pan with nonstick cooking spray.

2. Prepare cake mix according to package directions. Stir baking soda into mashed bananas; add to batter and beat until well blended. Spread batter in prepared pan.

3. Bake 30 to 35 minutes or until toothpick inserted into center comes out clean. Cool completely in pan on wire rack. *Makes 12 to 16 servings*

Lemon Blueberry Cake

   1 **package (about 18 ounces) lemon cake mix**
   1 **package (4-serving size) lemon instant pudding and pie filling mix**
   4 **eggs**
   ¾ **cup water**
   ½ **cup vegetable or canola oil**
   1 **cup fresh blueberries, divided**

1. Preheat oven to 350°F. Spray 13×9-inch baking pan with nonstick cooking spray.

2. Combine cake mix, pudding mix, eggs, water and oil in large bowl; beat 1 to 2 minutes or until well blended. Gently fold in ½ cup blueberries. Spread batter in prepared pan; sprinkle with remaining ½ cup blueberries.

3. Bake 20 to 25 minutes or until toothpick inserted into center comes out clean. Cool completely in pan on wire rack.   *Makes 12 to 16 servings*

CHOCOLATE
Heaven

Dark Chocolate Raspberry Dump Cake

- 1½ cups raspberry fruit spread or jam
- ½ cup dark chocolate chips, divided
- 1 package (about 15 ounces) dark chocolate cake mix
- ½ cup (1 stick) butter, cut into thin slices
- ¼ cup water

1. Preheat oven to 350°F. Spray 9-inch square baking pan with nonstick cooking spray.

2. Spread fruit spread evenly over bottom of prepared pan; sprinkle with ¼ cup chocolate chips. Top with cake mix, spreading evenly. Sprinkle with remaining ¼ cup chocolate chips. Top with butter in single layer, covering cake mix as much as possible. Drizzle water over top.

3. Bake 25 to 30 minutes or until toothpick inserted into center of cake comes out clean. Cool at least 15 minutes before serving.   *Makes 9 servings*

Chocolate Peanut Butter Cake

  1 **package (about 15 ounces) chocolate fudge cake mix**

1¼ **cups water**

  3 **eggs**

 ⅓ **cup vegetable or canola oil**

 ⅔ **cup creamy peanut butter, warmed,* divided**

  1 **cup unwrapped mini peanut butter cups**

*Microwave peanut butter on LOW (30%) about 2 minutes or until pourable.

1. Preheat oven to 350°F. Spray 13×9-inch baking pan with nonstick cooking spray.

2. Combine cake mix, water, eggs, oil and ⅓ cup peanut butter in large bowl; beat 1 to 2 minutes or until well blended. Spread batter in prepared pan. Drizzle with remaining ⅓ cup peanut butter; sprinkle with peanut butter cups.

3. Bake 25 to 30 minutes or until toothpick inserted into center comes out clean. Cool in pan at least 20 minutes before serving.

Makes 12 to 16 servings

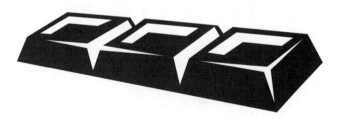

Strawberry Devil's Food Cake

1 **package (about 15 ounces) devil's food cake mix**
1 **can (21 ounces) strawberry pie filling**
3 **eggs**

1. Preheat oven to 350°F. Spray 13×9-inch baking pan with nonstick cooking spray.

2. Combine cake mix, strawberry pie filling and eggs in large bowl; beat 1 to 2 minutes or until well blended. Spread batter in prepared pan.

3. Bake 30 to 35 minutes or until toothpick inserted into center comes out clean. Cool completely in pan on wire rack. *Makes 12 to 16 servings*

Simply Delicious Chocolate Cake

- 1 cup Greek yogurt
- 1 cup coffee
- 1 package (about 15 ounces) chocolate cake mix
- 2 cups chopped creamy nougat and caramel candy bars, divided

1. Preheat oven to 350°F. Spray 13×9-inch baking pan with nonstick cooking spray.

2. Whisk yogurt and coffee in large bowl until blended. Add cake mix; beat 1 to 2 minutes or until well blended. Stir in 1 cup chopped candy. Spread batter in prepared pan; sprinkle with remaining 1 cup candy.

3. Bake 25 to 30 minutes or until toothpick inserted into center comes out clean. Cool completely in pan on wire rack. *Makes 12 to 16 servings*

Decadent Chocolate Delight

> 1 package (about 15 ounces) chocolate cake mix
> 1 package (4-serving size) chocolate instant pudding and pie filling mix
> 1 cup water
> 4 eggs
> 1 cup sour cream
> 1 cup semisweet chocolate chips
> ¾ cup vegetable or canola oil

1. Spray slow cooker with nonstick cooking spray.

2. Combine cake mix, pudding mix, water, eggs, sour cream, chocolate chips and oil in large bowl; beat until well blended. Transfer to slow cooker.

3. Cover; cook on LOW 3 to 4 hours or on HIGH 1½ to 1¾ hours. Serve warm.

Makes 12 servings

Chocolate Cinnamon Cake

   1 **package (about 15 ounces) devil's food cake mix**

1¼ **cups water**

   3 **eggs**

  ⅓ **cup vegetable or canola oil**

   1 **tablespoon instant coffee granules**

1½ **teaspoons ground cinnamon**

      Powdered sugar

1. Preheat oven to 350°F. Spray 13×9-inch baking pan with nonstick cooking spray.

2. Combine cake mix, water, eggs, oil, coffee granules and cinnamon in large bowl; beat 1 to 2 minutes or until well blended. Spread batter in prepared pan.

3. Bake 25 to 30 minutes or until toothpick inserted into center comes out clean. Cool completely in pan on wire rack.

4. Sprinkle with powdered sugar just before serving. *Makes 12 to 16 servings*

Chocolate Mystery Cake

  1 **package (about 15 ounces) German chocolate cake mix**
1½ **cups root beer (not diet)**
  2 **eggs**
 ¼ **cup vegetable or canola oil**
  1 **container (about 16 ounces) vanilla frosting**

1. Preheat oven to 350°F. Spray 13×9-inch baking pan with nonstick cooking spray.

2. Combine cake mix, root beer, eggs and oil in large bowl; beat 1 to 2 minutes or until well blended. Spread batter in prepared pan.

3. Bake 30 minutes or until toothpick inserted into center comes out clean. Cool completely in pan on wire rack.

4. Spread frosting over cooled cake.   *Makes 12 to 16 servings*

tip: For fluffy root beer-flavored frosting, beat frosting and 1 to 2 tablespoons root beer in medium bowl with electric mixer at medium speed about 2 minutes.

Cherry Chocolate Dump Cake

- 2 cans (21 ounces each) cherry pie filling
- 1 package (about 15 ounces) chocolate fudge cake mix
- ¾ cup semisweet chocolate chips
- ¾ cup (1½ sticks) butter, melted

1. Preheat oven to 350°F. Spray 13×9-inch baking pan with nonstick cooking spray.

2. Spread pie filling in prepared pan. Top with cake mix, spreading evenly. Sprinkle with chocolate chips. Pour butter over top, covering cake mix as much as possible.

3. Bake 30 to 35 minutes or until toothpick inserted into center of cake comes out clean. Cool at least 15 minutes before serving.

Makes 12 to 16 servings

Red Velvet Cake

1 package (about 18 ounces) red velvet cake mix
1 package (4-serving size) vanilla instant pudding and pie filling mix
1½ cups milk
2 ounces cream cheese, cut into small pieces
½ cup white chocolate chips

1. Preheat oven to 350°F. Spray 13×9-inch baking pan with nonstick cooking spray.

2. Combine cake mix, pudding mix and milk in large bowl; beat 1 to 2 minutes or until well blended. Spread in prepared pan; sprinkle with cream cheese and white chips.

3. Bake 25 to 30 minutes or until toothpick inserted into center comes out clean. Cool in pan on wire rack.   *Makes 12 to 16 servings*

Aztec Chocolate Cake

    1 package (about 15 ounces) dark chocolate cake mix
    1 teaspoon ground cinnamon
    ¼ teaspoon ground red pepper
    1⅓ cups water
    3 eggs
    ½ cup vegetable or canola oil
    1 teaspoon almond extract
      Bittersweet Chocolate Ganache (recipe follows, optional)

1. Preheat oven to 350°F. Spray 13×9-inch baking pan with nonstick cooking spray; line bottom of pan with parchment or waxed paper.

2. Combine cake mix, cinnamon and red pepper in large bowl; mix well. Stir in water, eggs, oil and almond extract; beat 1 to 2 minutes or until well blended. Spread in prepared pan.

3. Bake 36 to 40 minutes or until toothpick inserted into center comes out clean. Cool 15 minutes in pan; invert onto wire rack. Remove and discard parchment paper and invert onto another rack. Cool completely.

4. Prepare Bittersweet Chocolate Ganache, if desired. Pour over cake; spread evenly to cover. Let stand 30 minutes or until set.

Makes 12 to 16 servings

Bittersweet Chocolate Ganache: Bring ⅔ cup whipping cream to a simmer in small saucepan over medium heat; remove from heat. Add 6 ounces finely chopped chocolate; stir 3 to 5 minutes or until chocolate is completely melted and mixture is smooth. Cool 15 minutes or until slightly thickened, stirring occasionally.

Chocolate Banana Cake

1 package (about 15 ounces) chocolate cake mix, plus ingredients
   to prepare mix
2 bananas, mashed (about 1 heaping cup)
1 teaspoon baking soda

1. Preheat oven to 350°F. Spray 13×9-inch baking pan with nonstick cooking spray.

2. Prepare cake mix according to package directions. Stir baking soda into bananas; add to batter and beat until well blended. Spread batter in prepared pan.

3. Bake 25 to 30 minutes or until toothpick inserted into center comes out clean. Cool completely in pan on wire rack.   *Makes 12 to 16 servings*

Simple S'More Cake

Pictured on page 152

- 1 package (about 15 ounces) milk chocolate cake mix
- 1 package (4-serving size) chocolate instant pudding and pie filling mix
- 1½ cups milk
- 1 cup mini marshmallows
- 3 milk chocolate bars (1.55 ounces each), broken into ½-inch pieces
  or 1 cup milk chocolate chips
- 3 whole graham crackers, crumbled into ½-inch pieces

1. Preheat oven to 350°F. Spray 13×9-inch baking pan with nonstick cooking spray.

2. Combine cake mix, pudding mix and milk in large bowl; beat 1 to 2 minutes or until well blended. Spread batter in prepared pan.

3. Bake 30 to 35 minutes or until toothpick inserted into center comes out clean. *Turn oven to broil.*

4. Sprinkle marshmallows, chocolate and graham crackers over cake. Broil 6 inches from heat source 30 seconds to 1 minute or until marshmallows are golden brown. (Watch carefully to prevent burning.) Cool at least 5 minutes before serving.   *Makes 12 to 16 servings*

Apricot Double Chip Dump Cake

Pictured on page 153

- **2 cups apricot preserves or jam**
- **½ cup semisweet chocolate chips, divided**
- **½ cup white chocolate chips, divided**
- **1 package (about 15 ounces) yellow cake mix**
- **½ cup (1 stick) butter, cut into thin slices**
- **⅓ cup water**

1. Preheat oven to 350°F. Spray 9-inch square baking pan with nonstick cooking spray.

2. Spread preserves in prepared pan. Sprinkle with half of semisweet chips and half of white chips. Top with cake mix, spreading evenly. Top with butter in single layer, covering cake mix as much as possible. Sprinkle with remaining semisweet and white chips. Drizzle water over top.

3. Bake 50 to 55 minutes or until toothpick inserted into center of cake comes out clean. Cool at least 15 minutes before serving. *Makes 9 servings*

Cookie-Filled Chocolate Cake

1 package (about 15 ounces) chocolate fudge cake mix

1 package (4-serving size) chocolate instant pudding and pie filling mix

4 eggs

1 cup sour cream

½ cup water

⅓ cup vegetable or canola oil

½ (16-ounce) package refrigerated chocolate chip cookie dough

1. Preheat oven to 350°F. Spray 13×9-inch baking pan with nonstick cooking spray.

2. Combine cake mix, pudding mix, eggs, sour cream, water and oil in large bowl; beat 1 to 2 minutes or until well blended. Spread batter in prepared pan. Drop teaspoonfuls of cookie dough over batter.

3. Bake 30 to 35 minutes or until toothpick inserted into center comes out clean. Cool in pan at least 15 minutes before serving.

Makes 12 to 16 servings

Chocolatey Cherry Dump Cake

2 cans (14½ ounces each) tart cherries in water, drained

1 package (about 15 ounces) chocolate cake mix

1 can (12 ounces) 23-flavor cola

1. Preheat oven to 350°F. Spray 13×9-inch baking pan with nonstick cooking spray.

2. Spread cherries in prepared pan. Top with cake mix, spreading evenly. Pour cola over top, covering cake mix as much as possible.

3. Bake 35 to 40 minutes or until toothpick inserted into center of cake comes out clean. Cool at least 15 minutes before serving.

Makes 12 to 16 servings

Easy Turtle Cake

   1 **package (about 15 ounces) devil's food cake mix**
   1 **package (4-serving size) chocolate instant pudding and pie filling mix**
1½ **cups milk**
   1 **cup chopped caramels**
   1 **cup semisweet chocolate chips**
½ **cup pecan pieces**
½ **teaspoon coarse salt (optional)**

1. Preheat oven to 350°F. Spray 13×9-inch baking pan with nonstick cooking spray.

2. Combine cake mix, pudding mix and milk in large bowl; beat 1 to 2 minutes or until well blended. Spread batter in prepared pan; top with caramels, chocolate chips and pecans. Sprinkle with salt, if desired.

3. Bake 30 to 35 minutes or until toothpick inserted into center comes out clean. Cool in pan at least 15 minutes before serving.

Makes 12 to 16 servings

FALL
Flavors

Cranberry Apple Dump Cake

    1   can (21 ounces) apple pie filling
    1   can (14 ounces) whole berry cranberry sauce
    1   package (about 15 ounces) yellow cake mix
    ½   cup (1 stick) butter, cut into thin slices
    ½   cup chopped walnuts

1. Preheat oven to 350°F. Spray 13×9-inch baking pan with nonstick cooking spray

2. Spread apple pie filling in prepared pan; top with cranberry sauce. Top with cake mix, spreading evenly. Top with butter in single layer, covering cake mix as much as possible. Sprinkle with walnuts.

3. Bake 50 to 55 minutes or until toothpick inserted into center of cake comes out clean. Cool at least 15 minutes before serving.

Makes 12 to 16 servings

Carrot Spice Cake

1 **cup shredded carrots**

½ **cup raisins**

   Boiling water

1 **can (20 ounces) crushed pineapple, undrained**

1 **package (about 15 ounces) spice cake mix**

½ **cup (1 stick) butter, melted**

1. Place carrots and raisins in medium bowl; cover with boiling water. Let stand 10 minutes.

2. Preheat oven to 350°F. Spray 13×9-inch baking pan with nonstick cooking spray.

3. Spread pineapple in prepared pan. Drain carrots and raisins; mix with pineapple in pan. Top with cake mix, spreading evenly. Pour butter over top, covering cake mix as much as possible.

4. Bake 30 to 35 minutes or until toothpick inserted into center of cake comes out clean. Cool at least 15 minutes before serving.

Makes 12 to 16 servings

Sweet Potato Cake

- 1 can (29 ounces) sweet potatoes, drained
- 1 package (about 15 ounces) yellow cake mix
- 3 eggs
- 1½ teaspoons apple pie spice, plus additional for top of cake
- ⅔ cup chopped nuts, divided

1. Preheat oven to 350°F. Spray 13×9-inch baking pan with nonstick cooking spray.

2. Place sweet potatoes in large bowl; mash with fork. Add cake mix, eggs and 1½ teaspoons apple pie spice; beat 1 to 2 minutes or until well blended. Stir in ⅓ cup nuts. Spread batter in prepared pan; sprinkle with remaining ⅓ cup nuts and additional apple pie spice.

3. Bake 30 to 35 minutes or until toothpick inserted into center comes out clean. Cool in pan at least 15 minutes before serving.

Makes 12 to 16 servings

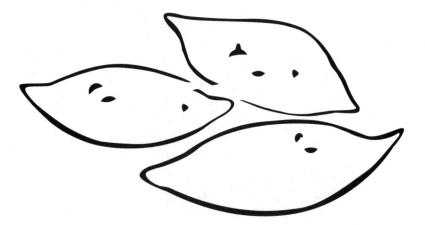

Apple Orchard Dump Cake

  6 cups sliced peeled Granny Smith apples (5 to 6 apples)

  ½ cup packed brown sugar

  2 teaspoons ground cinnamon

  ½ teaspoon ground nutmeg

  1 package (about 15 ounces) yellow cake mix

  ¾ cup (1½ sticks) butter, cut into thin slices

1. Preheat oven to 350°F. Spray 13×9-inch baking pan with nonstick cooking spray.

2. Combine apples, brown sugar, cinnamon and nutmeg in prepared pan; toss to coat. Spread in bottom of pan. Top with cake mix, spreading evenly. Top with butter in single layer, covering cake mix as much as possible.

3. Bake 50 to 55 minutes or until toothpick inserted into center of cake comes out clean. Cool at least 15 minutes before serving.

Makes 12 to 16 servings

Cranberry Pear Cake

Pictured on page 154

- 1 can (29 ounces) pear slices in light syrup, undrained
- 1 package (12 ounces) fresh or thawed frozen cranberries
- 1 package (about 15 ounces) spice cake mix
- ½ cup (1 stick) butter, cut into thin slices
- 1 cup chopped walnuts

1. Preheat oven to 350°F. Spray 13×9-inch baking pan with nonstick cooking spray.

2. Drain ½ cup liquid from pears. Pour pears and remaining liquid into prepared pan; cut pears into ½-inch pieces with paring knife or scissors. Spread cranberries over pears. Top with cake mix, spreading evenly. Top with butter in single layer, covering cake mix as much as possible. Sprinkle with walnuts.

3. Bake 40 to 45 minutes or until toothpick inserted into center of cake comes out clean. Cool at least 15 minutes before serving.

Makes 12 to 16 servings

Winter Squash Cake

- 1 package (about 15 ounces) yellow cake mix
- 1 package (14 ounces) frozen squash, thawed
- 2 eggs
- ¼ cup water
- 1 teaspoon ground cinnamon
- ½ teaspoon ground ginger
- ¾ cup raisins
- ½ cup chopped walnuts

1. Preheat oven to 350°F. Spray 13×9-inch baking pan with nonstick cooking spray.

2. Combine cake mix, squash, eggs, water, cinnamon and ginger in large bowl; beat 1 to 2 minutes or until well blended. Stir in raisins and walnuts. Spread batter in prepared pan.

3. Bake 25 to 30 minutes or until toothpick inserted into center comes out clean. Cool in pan at least 15 minutes before serving.

Makes 12 to 16 servings

Applesauce Spice Cake

  1 **package (about 15 ounces) spice cake mix**

1½ **cups applesauce**

  3 **eggs**

  1 **cup chopped walnuts**

 ¾ **cup raisins**

     Caramel topping or cream cheese frosting, warmed (optional)

1. Preheat oven to 350°F. Grease and flour 12-cup (10-inch) bundt pan.

2. Combine cake mix, applesauce and eggs in large bowl; beat 1 to 2 minutes or until well blended. Stir in walnuts and raisins. Pour batter into prepared pan.

3. Bake 30 to 35 minutes or until toothpick inserted near center comes out clean. Cool in pan 10 minutes; invert onto wire rack to cool completely. Drizzle with caramel topping or cream cheese frosting, if desired.

Makes 12 servings

Pumpkin Pecan Cake

Pictured on page 155

- 1 can (15 ounces) solid-pack pumpkin
- 1 can (12 ounces) evaporated milk
- 1 cup packed brown sugar
- 3 eggs
- 2 teaspoons pumpkin pie spice
- ½ teaspoon salt
- 1 package (about 15 ounces) yellow cake mix
- ¾ cup (1½ sticks) butter, cut into thin slices
- ½ cup pecan halves

1. Preheat oven to 350°F. Spray 13×9-inch baking pan with nonstick cooking spray.

2. Combine pumpkin, evaporated milk, brown sugar, eggs, pumpkin pie spice and salt in medium bowl; stir until well blended. Pour into prepared pan; top with cake mix, spreading evenly. Top with butter in single layer, covering cake mix as much as possible. Sprinkle with pecans.

3. Bake about 1 hour or until toothpick inserted into center of cake comes out clean. Cool completely in pan on wire rack.   *Makes 18 servings*

Autumn Dump Cake

Pictured on page 156

- **1 can (29 ounces) pear slices in light syrup, undrained**
- **1 can (21 ounces) apple pie filling**
- **½ cup dried cranberries**
- **1 package (about 15 ounces) yellow cake mix**
- **½ cup (1 stick) butter, cut into thin slices**
- **¼ cup caramel topping, warmed**

1. Preheat oven to 350°F. Spray 13×9-inch baking pan with nonstick cooking spray.

2. Drain pears, reserving syrup. Spread pears and apple pie filling in prepared pan; add ½ cup reserved syrup. Sprinkle with cranberries. Top with cake mix, spreading evenly. Top with butter in single layer, covering cake mix as much as possible. Drizzle with caramel topping.

3. Bake 40 to 45 minutes or until toothpick inserted into center of cake comes out clean. Cool at least 15 minutes before serving.

Makes 12 to 16 servings

Granola Caramel Carrot Cake

  1 can (20 ounces) crushed pineapple, undrained
  1 package (about 15 ounces) carrot cake mix
  ½ cup (1 stick) butter, cut into thin slices
  1 cup granola
  3 tablespoons caramel topping, warmed

1. Preheat oven to 350°F. Spray 13×9-inch baking pan with nonstick cooking spray.

2. Spread pineapple in prepared pan. Top with cake mix, spreading evenly. Top with butter in single layer, covering cake mix as much as possible. Sprinkle with granola; drizzle with caramel topping.

3. Bake 50 to 55 minutes or until toothpick inserted into center of cake comes out clean. Cool at least 15 minutes before serving.

Makes 12 to 16 servings

Cranberry Cobbler Cake

1 can (14 ounces) whole berry cranberry sauce

1 package (9 ounces) yellow cake mix

¼ cup (½ stick) butter, melted

½ cup granola

1. Preheat oven to 350°F. Spray 9-inch pie plate with nonstick cooking spray.

2. Spread cranberry sauce in prepared pie plate. Top with cake mix, spreading evenly. Pour butter over top, covering cake mix as much as possible. Sprinkle with granola.

3. Bake 55 to 60 minutes or until toothpick inserted into center of cake comes out clean. Cool at least 15 minutes before serving.

Makes 6 to 8 servings

Triple Ginger Pear Cake

- 2 cans (29 ounces each) pear slices in light syrup, undrained
- ⅓ cup finely chopped crystallized ginger
- ¼ teaspoon ground ginger
- 1 package (about 15 ounces) yellow cake mix
- ½ cup (1 stick) butter, cut into thin slices
- 1 cup crumbled gingersnaps (about 16 cookies)

1. Preheat oven to 350°F. Spray 13×9-inch baking pan with nonstick cooking spray.

2. Drain pears, reserving 1 cup syrup. Cut pears into ¾-inch chunks with paring knife or scissors. Combine pears and reserved syrup in prepared pan; sprinkle with crystallized ginger and ground ginger. Top with cake mix, spreading evenly. Top with butter in single layer, covering cake mix as much as possible. Sprinkle with crumbled gingersnaps.

3. Bake 40 to 45 minutes or until toothpick inserted into center of cake comes out clean. Cool at least 15 minutes before serving.

Makes 12 to 16 servings

Caramel Apple Peanut Cake

Pictured on page 157

- **2** cans (21 ounces each) apple pie filling
- **½** cup lightly salted peanuts, divided
- **1** package (about 15 ounces) yellow cake mix
- **½** cup (1 stick) butter, cut into thin slices
- **⅓** cup caramel topping, warmed

1. Preheat oven to 350°F. Spray 13×9-inch baking pan with nonstick cooking spray.

2. Spread apple pie filling in prepared pan; sprinkle with ¼ cup peanuts. Top with cake mix, spreading evenly. Top with butter in single layer, covering cake mix as much as possible. Drizzle with caramel topping; sprinkle with remaining ¼ cup peanuts.

3. Bake 35 to 40 minutes or until toothpick inserted into center of cake comes out clean. Cool at least 15 minutes before serving.

Makes 12 to 16 servings

Pumpkin Chocolate Chip Cake

    1 **package (about 15 ounces) spice cake mix**

    1 **can (15 ounces) solid-pack pumpkin**

    2 **eggs**

  ⅓ **cup water**

    1 **cup semisweet chocolate chips**

    1 **cup semisweet chocolate chips, melted (optional)**

1. Preheat oven to 350°F. Grease and flour 12-cup (10-inch) bundt pan.

2. Combine cake mix, pumpkin, eggs and water in large bowl; beat 1 to 2 minutes or until well blended. Stir in chocolate chips. Pour batter into prepared pan.

3. Bake 35 to 40 minutes or until toothpick inserted near center comes out clean. Cool in pan 10 minutes; invert onto wire rack to cool completely.

4. Drizzle melted chocolate over cooled cake, if desired.   *Makes 12 servings*

Orange Cranberry Cake

  1 **package (about 15 ounces) yellow cake mix**

  4 **eggs**

  ¾ **cup fresh orange juice**

  ½ **cup vegetable or canola oil**

  ¼ **cup water**

  1 **cup dried cranberries**

     Powdered sugar (optional)

1. Preheat oven to 350°F. Grease and flour 12-cup (10-inch) bundt pan.

2. Combine cake mix, eggs, orange juice, oil and water in large bowl; beat 1 to 2 minutes or until well blended. Stir in cranberries. Pour batter into prepared pan.

3. Bake about 35 minutes or until toothpick inserted near center comes out clean. Cool in pan 10 minutes; invert onto wire rack to cool completely.

4. Sprinkle with powdered sugar just before serving, if desired.

Makes 12 servings

TROPICAL
Treats

Island Delight Cake
Pictured on page 158

3 ripe mangoes, peeled and cubed (about 4½ cups)

1 package (about 18 ounces) pineapple cake mix

1 can (12 ounces) lemon-lime or orange soda

½ cup chopped macadamia nuts (optional)

1. Preheat oven to 350°F. Spray 13×9-inch baking pan with nonstick cooking spray.

2. Spread mangoes in prepared pan. Top with cake mix, spreading evenly. Pour soda over top, covering cake mix as much as possible. Sprinkle with macadamia nuts, if desired.

3. Bake 35 to 40 minutes or until toothpick inserted into center of cake comes out clean. Cool at least 15 minutes before serving.

Makes 12 to 16 servings

Pineapple Right Side Up Cake

1 can (20 ounces) crushed pineapple, undrained

1 cup coarsely chopped maraschino cherries

1 package (about 15 ounces) yellow cake mix

½ cup (1 stick) butter, cut into thin slices

1. Preheat oven to 350°F. Spray 13×9-inch baking pan with nonstick cooking spray.

2. Spread pineapple in prepared pan; sprinkle with cherries. Top with cake mix, spreading evenly. Top with butter in single layer, covering cake mix as much as possible.

3. Bake 35 to 40 minutes or until toothpick inserted into center of cake comes out clean. Cool at least 15 minutes before serving.

Makes 12 to 16 servings

Orange Coconut Cake

　　1　can (20 ounces) crushed pineapple, undrained
　　1　can (15 ounces) mandarin oranges in light syrup, drained
1½　cups flaked coconut, divided
　　1　package (about 15 ounces) vanilla cake mix
　½　cup (1 stick) butter, cut into thin slices

1. Preheat oven to 350°F. Spray 13×9-inch baking pan with nonstick cooking spray.

2. Spread pineapple and mandarin oranges in prepared pan; sprinkle with ½ cup coconut. Top with cake mix, spreading evenly. Top with butter in single layer, covering cake mix as much as possible. Sprinkle with remaining 1 cup coconut.

3. Bake 45 to 50 minutes or until toothpick inserted into center of cake comes out clean. Cool at least 15 minutes before serving.

Makes 12 to 16 servings

Fruit-Filled Dump Cake

  1 **can (20 ounces) crushed pineapple, undrained**
  1 **package (12 ounces) frozen peach slices, thawed and drained**
  1 **cup fresh or thawed frozen sliced strawberries**
  1 **package (about 18 ounces) banana cake mix**
  ½ **cup tropical dried fruit mix**
  ½ **cup (1 stick) butter, melted**

1. Preheat oven to 350°F. Spray 13×9-inch baking pan with nonstick cooking spray.

2. Spread pineapple, peaches and strawberries in prepared pan. Top with cake mix, spreading evenly. Sprinkle with dried fruit. Pour butter over top, covering cake mix as much as possible.

3. Bake 50 to 55 minutes or until toothpick inserted into center of cake comes out clean. Cool at least 15 minutes before serving.

Makes 12 to 16 servings

Pineapple Blueberry Upside Down Cake

¼ cup (½ stick) butter, melted

½ cup packed brown sugar

1 can (20 ounces) crushed pineapple, drained

2 cups thawed frozen blueberries

1 package (about 18 ounces) pineapple cake mix, plus ingredients to prepare mix

1. Preheat oven to 350°F. Spray two 9-inch round cake pans with nonstick cooking spray.

2. Divide butter and brown sugar between prepared pans; spread evenly over bottoms of pans. Spread pineapple and blueberries evenly over butter mixture.

3. Prepare cake mix according to package directions. Spread batter over fruit in each pan.

4. Bake 25 to 30 minutes or until toothpick inserted into center of cakes comes out clean. Cool 5 minutes; invert onto serving plates. Serve warm or at room temperature. *Makes 12 to 16 servings*

Double Pineapple Berry Cake

Pictured on page 159

- 1 can (20 ounces) crushed pineapple, undrained
- 1 package (12 ounces) frozen mixed berries, thawed and drained
- 1 package (about 18 ounces) pineapple cake mix
- ½ cup (1 stick) butter, cut into thin slices

1. Preheat oven to 350°F. Spray 13×9-inch baking pan with nonstick cooking spray.

2. Spread pineapple and berries in prepared pan. Top with cake mix, spreading evenly. Top with butter in single layer, covering cake mix as much as possible.

3. Bake 45 to 50 minutes or until toothpick inserted into center of cake comes out clean. Cool at least 15 minutes before serving.

Makes 12 to 16 servings

Tropical Dump Cake

Pictured on page 160

- 1 can (20 ounces) crushed pineapple, undrained
- 1 can (15 ounces) peach slices, undrained
- 1 package (about 15 ounces) yellow cake mix
- ½ cup (1 stick butter), cut into thin slices
- 1 cup packed brown sugar
- ½ cup flaked coconut
- ½ cup chopped pecans

1. Preheat oven to 350°F. Spray 13×9-inch pan with nonstick cooking spray.

2. Spread pineapple and peaches in prepared pan. Top with cake mix, spreading evenly. Top with butter in single layer, covering cake mix as much as possible. Sprinkle with brown sugar, coconut and pecans.

3. Bake 40 to 45 minutes or until toothpick inserted into center of cake comes out clean. Cool at least 15 minutes before serving.

Makes 12 to 16 servings

Taste of the Tropics Cake

- 1 can (20 ounces) crushed pineapple, undrained
- 2 cups fresh mango cubes (½-inch pieces)
- 1 package (about 18 ounces) banana cake mix
- ½ cup (1 stick) butter, cut into thin slices
- 1 cup chopped walnuts
- ¾ cup flaked coconut

1. Preheat oven to 350°F. Spray 13×9-inch baking pan with nonstick cooking spray.

2. Spread pineapple and mangoes in prepared pan. Top with cake mix, spreading evenly. Top with butter in single layer, covering cake mix as much as possible. Sprinkle with walnuts and coconut.

3. Bake 50 to 55 minutes or until toothpick inserted into center of cake comes out clean. Cool at least 15 minutes before serving.

Makes 12 to 16 servings

Pineapple Angel Cake

  2 **cups fresh or thawed frozen sliced strawberries**
  1 **can (20 ounces) crushed pineapple, undrained**
  1 **package (16 ounces) angel food cake mix**

1. Preheat oven to 350°F.

2. Spread strawberries in 13×9-inch baking pan. Combine pineapple and cake mix in large bowl; beat 1 to 2 minutes or until well blended. Pour batter evenly over strawberries.

3. Bake 35 to 40 minutes or until toothpick inserted into center comes out clean. Cool at least 30 minutes before serving.   *Makes 12 to 16 servings*

Sweet-Tart Lemon Pineapple Cake

1 can (about 16 ounces) lemon pie filling

1 can (20 ounces) crushed pineapple, undrained

1 package (about 15 ounces) lemon cake mix

¾ cup (1½ sticks) butter, cut into thin slices

¾ cup chopped macadamia nuts

¾ cup flaked coconut

1. Preheat oven to 350°F. Spray 13×9-inch baking pan with nonstick cooking spray.

2. Spread lemon pie filling in prepared pan; top with pineapple. Top with cake mix, spreading evenly. Top with butter in single layer, covering cake mix as much as possible. Sprinkle with macadamia nuts and coconut.

3. Bake 50 to 55 minutes or until toothpick inserted into center of cake comes out clean. Cool at least 15 minutes before serving.

Makes 12 to 16 servings

Mango Piña Colada Cake

- 1 can (20 ounces) crushed pineapple, undrained
- 1 cup frozen mango chunks, thawed (cut any large chunks into smaller pieces)
- 1 package (about 15 ounces) white cake mix
- 1 cup full-fat coconut milk,* well shaken

Do not use low-fat or reduced-fat coconut milk in this recipe.

1. Preheat oven to 350°F. Spray 13×9-inch baking pan with nonstick cooking spray.

2. Spread pineapple and mango in prepared pan. Top with cake mix, spreading evenly. Pour coconut milk over top, covering cake mix as much as possible.

3. Bake 45 to 50 minutes or until toothpick inserted into center of cake comes out clean. Cool at least 15 minutes before serving.

Makes 12 to 16 servings

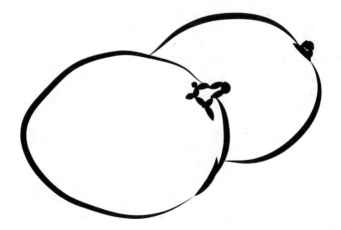

CATHY'S
Cakes & More

Cherry Dump Cake

    1   package (about 15 ounces) yellow or white cake mix
    1   can (21 ounces) cherry pie filling
    1   can (20 ounces) crushed pineapple, undrained
    ½   cup (1 stick) butter, melted
    ½   cup chopped pecans (optional)

1. Preheat oven to 350°F. Spray 13×9-inch baking pan with nonstick cooking spray.

2. Spread cherry pie filling in bottom of prepared pan. Add pineapple with juice; mix with cherries and spread evenly. Top with dry cake mix, carefully spreading over fruit layer with fork. Do not mix.

3. Drizzle butter over cake mix, covering as much as possible. Sprinkle with pecans, if desired.

4. Bake 40 to 45 minutes or until golden brown. Cool 15 to 30 minutes. Serve warm.   *Makes 12 servings*

Simply Scrumptious Apple Cake

1 package (about 16 ounces) angel food cake*

1 can (21 ounces) regular or no-sugar-added apple pie filling (see Tip)

1 teaspoon ground cinnamon

3 tablespoons packed brown sugar

¼ cup chopped walnuts

Use a one-step angel food cake mix that requires only water.

1. Preheat oven to 350°F. Spray 13×9-inch baking pan with nonstick cooking spray.

2. Combine dry cake mix, apple pie filling and cinnamon in large bowl. (Batter will thicken up during mixing; do not overmix.) Spread batter in prepared pan; sprinkle with brown sugar and walnuts.

3. Bake 30 minutes. Cool in pan 20 to 30 minutes. Serve warm.

Makes 12 servings

tip: Use a sharp knife to cut through the apples while still in the can so you have smaller pieces without any mess.

S'More Magic Bars

1½ cups finely crushed graham crackers (about 1 sleeve)

½ cup (1 stick) butter, melted

1 can (14 ounces) sweetened condensed milk

1 cup milk chocolate chips

1 cup mini marshmallows

6 chocolate sandwich cookies, crushed

1. Preheat oven to 350°F. Line 13×9-inch baking pan with foil; spray with nonstick cooking spray.

2. Combine graham cracker crumbs and butter in medium bowl; mix with fork until crumbly. Press evenly into prepared pan to form crust.

3. Pour sweetened condensed milk evenly over crust. Top with chocolate chips, marshmallows and crushed cookies.

4. Bake 20 to 25 minutes or until marshmallows are lightly browned. Cool in pan 20 to 30 minutes. Remove foil from pan; cut into bars.

Makes 18 bars

Easy Pineapple Cake

So simple and diet friendly!

  1 **package (about 16 ounces) angel food cake mix***
  1 **can (20 ounces) crushed pineapple, undrained**
  ⅓ **cup shredded or flaked coconut (optional)**

*Use a one-step angel food cake mix that requires only water.

1. Preheat oven to 350°F. Spray 13×9-inch baking pan with nonstick cooking spray.

2. Place dry cake mix in large bowl; stir in pineapple with juice using rubber spatula. (Mixture will foam and expand, resembling marshmallow crème.) Spread batter evenly in prepared pan; sprinkle with coconut, if desired.

3. Bake 25 to 30 minutes or until cake is set and coconut is lightly browned. Serve warm.

Makes 12 servings

Tip: This cake makes a great base for strawberry shortcake.

Cookies and Cream Bars

½ cup (1 stick) butter, melted
1 package (about 15 ounces) chocolate cake mix
1 egg, beaten *or* ¼ cup egg substitute
12 chocolate sandwich cookies, coarsely crushed
1 can (14 ounces) sweetened condensed milk
1 package (12 ounces) chocolate chips

1. Preheat oven to 350°F. Spray 13×9-inch baking pan with nonstick cooking spray.

2. Pour butter evenly over bottom of prepared pan. Cover with dry cake mix and drizzle with egg; stir with fork until moistened. (Or mix butter, cake mix and egg in large bowl until crumbly.) Press mixture into bottom of pan with fingers to form thick crust.

3. Top crust with cookies. Slowly pour sweetened condensed milk over cookies, covering as evenly as possible. Sprinkle with chocolate chips.

4. Bake 25 to 30 minutes or until set. Cool 5 minutes; cut into bars.

Makes 12 bars

Razzleberry Lemon Cake

3 to 4 cups fresh raspberries or mixed berries

1 can (12 ounces) diet lemon-lime soda

1 package (4-serving size) raspberry gelatin (regular or sugar-free)

1 package (about 18 ounces) lemon cake mix

½ cup (1 stick) butter, melted

1. Preheat oven to 350°F. Spray 13×9-inch baking pan with nonstick cooking spray.

2. Spread raspberries in bottom of prepared pan. Pour soda over raspberries; sprinkle with dry gelatin. Top with dry cake mix, carefully spreading over fruit layer with fork. Do not mix. Drizzle butter over cake mix, covering as much as possible.

3. Bake 45 to 60 minutes or until top is golden and cake is set. Cool 15 to 30 minutes. Serve warm.

Makes 12 servings

Caramel Apple Cake

- 1 package (about 15 ounces) yellow cake mix
- 2 cans (21 ounces each) apple pie filling
- ½ cup caramel sauce
- 1 teaspoon ground cinnamon
- ½ cup (1 stick) butter, melted
- Chopped pecans (optional)
- Ice cream or whipped cream and additional caramel sauce (optional)

1. Preheat oven to 350°F. Spray 13×9-inch baking pan with nonstick cooking spray.

2. Spread apple pie filling evenly in bottom of prepared pan. Sprinkle with cinnamon; drizzle evenly with caramel sauce. Top with dry cake mix, carefully spreading over apples with fork. Do not mix. Drizzle butter over cake mix, covering as much as possible. Sprinkle with pecans, if desired.

3. Bake 30 to 40 minutes or until top is golden and cake is set. Cool 15 to 30 minutes. Serve warm with ice cream or whipped cream and additional caramel sauce, if desired.

Makes 12 servings

Triple Chocolate Cake

A little mixing but worth it!

     1 **package (about 15 ounces) chocolate cake mix**
     1 **package (4-serving size) chocolate instant pudding and pie filling mix**
     1 **package (12 ounces) chocolate chips**
  1½ **cups milk**

1. Preheat oven to 350°F. Spray 13×9-inch baking pan with nonstick cooking spray.

2. Dump cake mix, pudding mix and milk in large bowl; stir until well blended. (Mixture will be very thick.) Spread evenly in prepared pan; sprinkle with chocolate chips.

3. Bake 30 minutes. Cool completely in pan.   *Makes 12 servings*

Sticky Bun Breakfast Ring

     1 **tube (about 16 ounces) jumbo buttermilk biscuit dough (8 biscuits)**
   ⅓ **cup packed brown sugar**
   ½ **teaspoon ground cinnamon**
   ¼ **cup sliced almonds**
   ½ **cup pancake syrup, divided**
     3 **tablespoons butter, melted, divided**

1. Preheat oven to 375°F. Spray bundt pan with nonstick cooking spray. Combine brown sugar, cinnamon and almonds in small bowl.

2. Pour half of syrup and half of butter into prepared pan; sprinkle with half of brown sugar mixture. Place biscuits over brown sugar mixture, overlapping to form ring. Top with remaining syrup, butter and brown sugar mixture.

3. Bake 20 to 25 minutes or until golden brown. Cool in pan 1 minute; invert onto serving platter.   *Makes 8 servings*

Black Forest Cake

   1 **can (21 ounces) cherry pie filling***

   1 **can (15 ounces) pitted dark cherries,* drained**

   1 **package (about 15 ounces) German chocolate cake mix**

   1 **can (12 ounces) cherry cola (regular or diet)**

      Ice cream or whipped cream and chocolate sauce (optional)

*Or use two of either kind of cherries instead of one of each.

1. Preheat oven to 350°F. Spray 13×9-inch baking pan with nonstick cooking spray.

2. Spread cherry pie filling and cherries in bottom of prepared pan. Top with dry cake mix, carefully spreading over cherries with fork. Do not mix. Slowly pour soda over cake mix, covering as much as possible. Do not mix.

3. Cover with foil and bake 20 minutes. Remove foil; bake additional 30 to 40 minutes or until cake is set. Cool 15 minutes. Serve warm with ice cream or whipped cream and chocolate sauce, if desired.   *Makes 12 servings*

Raz and Peach Cobbler

So fresh tasting and not overly sweet!

- **1 package (16 ounces) frozen peaches**
- **1 package (12 ounces) ounces frozen raspberries *or* 1 container (8 ounces) fresh raspberries**
- **1 package (about 15 ounces) yellow cake mix**
- **1 can (12 ounces) diet lemon-lime soda**
- **Vanilla frozen yogurt (optional)**

1. Preheat oven to 350°F. Spray 13×9-inch baking pan with nonstick cooking spray.

2. Spread frozen peaches and raspberries in bottom of prepared pan. Top with dry cake mix, carefully spreading over peaches with fork. Do not mix. Slowly pour soda over cake mix, covering as much as possible. Do not mix.

3. Cover with foil and bake 20 minutes. Remove foil; bake additional 40 minutes. Cool 20 minutes. Serve warm with frozen yogurt, if desired.

Makes 12 servings

Basic Mug Cake

Sometimes called 3-2-1 Cake.

> 1 package (about 15 ounces) cake mix, any flavor
>
> 1 package (16 ounces) angel food cake mix*

*Use a one-step angel food cake mix that requires only water.

1. Combine dry cake mixes in canister with lid.

2. To make mug cake, combine 3 tablespoons dry mix and 2 tablespoons water in microwavable mug; mix well.

3. Microwave on HIGH 1 minute. (Adjust cooking time as needed based on wattage of microwave.)   *Makes 36 cakes*

Variations: Add 1 teaspoon unsweetened cocoa powder for chocolate cake. Substitute cold coffee or fruit juice for water for mocha- or fruit-flavored cakes. Top hot cake with chocolate chips, mini marshmallows, chocolate hazelnut spread or peanut butter to create instant frosting.

Pineapple Upside Dump Cake

> 1 teaspoon butter, softened or melted
>
> 1 to 2 tablespoons packed brown sugar
>
> 1 pineapple ring
>
> 1 maraschino cherry
>
> 6 tablespoons Basic Mug Cake mix (recipe above)
>
> 4 tablespoons pineapple juice or water

1. Spray large microwavable mug with nonstick cooking spray.

2. Place butter in mug and top with brown sugar. Place pineapple ring over sugar and place cherry in center.

3. Stir cake mix and juice until blended. Carefully pour over pineapple.

4. Microwave on HIGH 1 minute or until toothpick inserted into center comes out clean. Add additional time if necessary. Let stand 1 minute before inverting onto plate. Serve warm.   *Makes 1 serving*

Pudding Mug Cake

A moister version of the basic mug cake.

1 package (about 15 ounces) cake mix, any flavor

1 package (about 16 ounces) angel food cake mix*

2 packages (4-serving size) instant pudding and pie filling mix, any flavor

Use a one-step angel food cake mix that requires only water.

1. Combine dry cake mixes and pudding mix in canister with lid.

2. To make mug cake, combine ¼ cup dry mix and ¼ cup water in microwavable mug; mix well.

3. Microwave on HIGH 1 minute. (Adjust cooking time as needed based on wattage of microwave.)   *Makes 36 cakes*

Try any of the following combinations: Chocolate cake mix with chocolate pudding, yellow cake mix with vanilla pudding or yellow cake mix with butterscotch pudding.

Variations: Substitute cold coffee or fruit juice for water for mocha- or fruit-flavored cakes. Stir in canned fruit, coconut, chocolate chips, nuts, crushed pretzels, crushed chocolate sandwich cookies or other cookies immediately after cooking. Top hot cake with chocolate chips, mini marshmallows, chocolate hazelnut spread or peanut butter to create instant frosting.

Cup o' Apple Pie

- 1 small apple, peeled, cored and chopped
- 1 tablespoon brown sugar
- 1 teaspoon old-fashioned or quick oats*
- ½ teaspoon ground cinnamon
- 1 thin pat butter
  Ice cream or whipped cream (optional)

*Or substitute 1 heaping tablespoon instant oatmeal mix (from cup or package); reduce amount of sugar.

1. Place apples in microwavable mug. Stir in brown sugar, oats and cinnamon. Top with butter.

2. Microwave on HIGH 1½ to 2 minutes or until apple is tender. (Time will vary depending on wattage of microwave and thickness of apple pieces.) Stir mixture; top with ice cream or whipped cream, if desired.

Makes 1 serving

S'Mores in a Mug

Same great taste, no campfire needed!

> **2** **whole graham crackers (rectangles), divided**
>
> **20** **mini marshmallows**
>
> **3** **tablespoons milk chocolate chips**

1. Spray inside of microwavable mug with nonstick cooking spray

2. Crush 1 graham cracker into bottom of mug; top with marshmallows and chocolate chips. Crush remaining graham cracker; sprinkle over chocolate chips.

3. Microwave on HIGH 30 seconds. (Mixture will puff up inside mug.) Stir to melt chocolate. *Makes 1 serving*

Coffee Cup Coffeecake

⅓ cup biscuit baking mix

¼ cup milk

1 pat butter, divided

2 rounded teaspoons Brown Sugar Mix (recipe follows), divided

1. Spray inside of microwavable coffee cup with nonstick cooking spray

2. Combine baking mix and milk in prepared cup; mix well with large spoon. Scoop up half of mixture with spoon. Sprinkle 1 teaspoon Brown Sugar mix over dough in cup; top with ½ pat of butter. Replace spoonful of dough in cup; top with remaining 1 teaspoon Brown Sugar Mix and ½ pat of butter.

3. Microwave on HIGH 1 minute. Turn coffeecake onto plate or eat from cup.

Makes 1 serving

Brown Sugar Mix: Combine ¼ cup packed brown sugar, 2 tablespoons chopped nuts, if desired, and 1 teaspoon ground cinnamon in small bowl; mix well. Store in covered container. Makes enough for 4 coffeecakes.

S'Mores Chocolate Cake in a Skillet

Less calories than an ordinary frosted cake!

- **1 can (12 ounces) diet soda**
- **1 package (about 15 ounces) chocolate cake mix**
- **½ cup milk chocolate chips**
- **½ cup mini marshmallows**
- **½ cup coarsely chopped pecans**
- **2 chocolate sandwich cookies, broken into pieces *or* 2 packages mini chocolate sandwich cookies**

1. Preheat oven to 350°F. Spray 12-inch ovenproof skillet with nonstick cooking spray.

2. Pour soda into skillet. Add cake mix and stir with plastic whisk or spatula until blended. (Or mix soda and cake mix in large bowl.)

3. Spread batter evenly in prepared skillet. Top evenly with chocolate chips, marshmallows, pecans and cookies.

4. Bake 30 minutes or until toothpick inserted into center comes out clean. Cool at least 15 minutes before serving. *Makes 10 servings*

Serving Suggestion: Serve warm with a scoop of vanilla ice cream.

Variations: Try different toppings on the cake, such as flaked coconut, mini graham crackers, chopped candy bars, peanut butter or butterscotch chips, salted peanuts or favorite breakfast cereals.

QUICK-TO-FIX
Cakes

Blueberry Coconut Cake

- 1 cup packed brown sugar
- 6 tablespoons butter, melted
- 1 tablespoon white vinegar
- 1 teaspoon vanilla
- ¾ cup all-purpose flour
- ¾ cup whole wheat flour
- 1 teaspoon baking soda
- ½ teaspoon ground cinnamon
- ¼ teaspoon salt
- 1¼ cups sour cream
- 1 cup flaked coconut, toasted*
- ¾ cup dried blueberries

*To toast coconut, spead on baking sheet. Bake at 350°F about 2 minutes or until golden brown.

1. Preheat oven to 350°F. Spray 9-inch square baking pan with nonstick cooking spray.

2. Combine brown sugar, butter, vinegar and vanilla in large bowl; mix well. Stir in all-purpose flour, whole wheat flour, baking soda, cinnamon and salt until blended. Add sour cream; mix well. Stir in coconut and blueberries. Spread batter in prepared pan.

3. Bake 35 minutes or until toothpick inserted into center comes out clean. Cool completely in pan on wire rack. *Makes 9 servings*

Apple Cake

  4 cups diced peeled green apples
  2 cups sugar
  ½ cup vegetable or canola oil
  2 eggs
  2 cups all-purpose flour
  2 teaspoons baking soda
  2 teaspoons ground cinnamon
  1 teaspoon salt
  1 teaspoon ground nutmeg
  ½ cup chopped walnuts

1. Preheat oven to 350°F. Spray 13×9-inch baking pan with nonstick cooking spray.

2. Combine apples, sugar, oil and eggs in large bowl; mix well. Add flour, baking soda, cinnamon, salt and nutmeg; stir until well blended. Stir in walnuts. Spread batter in prepared pan.

3. Bake 1 hour or until toothpick inserted into center comes out clean.

Makes 12 to 16 servings

Citrusy Pound Cakes

2 packages (16 ounces each) pound cake mix

4 eggs

1 cup water

½ cup orange juice

2 tablespoons lemon juice

2 teaspoons grated lemon peel

2 teaspoons grated orange peel

Citrus Glaze (recipe follows, optional)

1. Preheat oven to 350°F. Spray six small (5×3-inch) loaf pans with nonstick cooking spray. Place on baking sheet.

2. Combine cake mix, eggs, water, orange juice, lemon juice, lemon peel and orange peel in large bowl; beat 2 minutes or until well blended. Pour 1 cup batter into each prepared pan.

3. Bake 45 minutes or until toothpick inserted into centers comes out clean. Cool completely in pans on wire racks.

4. Prepare Citrus Glaze, if desired. Drizzle over cooled cakes; let stand until set.

Makes 6 small cakes

Citrus Glaze: Combine 1 cup powdered sugar, 1 tablespoon orange or lemon juice and ½ teaspoon vanilla in small bowl; whisk until smooth. Add additional juice, if necessary, to reach desired consistency.

Chocolate Peanut Butter Oatmeal Snack Cake

1¼ cups boiling water

1 cup old-fashioned oats

1 cup granulated sugar

1 cup packed brown sugar

½ cup (1 stick) butter, softened

2 eggs

1 teaspoon vanilla

1¾ cups all-purpose flour

¼ cup unsweetened cocoa powder

1 teaspoon baking soda

1 cup semisweet chocolate chips

1 package (12 ounces) chocolate and peanut butter chips

1. Preheat oven to 350°F. Spray 13×9-inch baking pan with nonstick cooking spray.

2. Combine boiling water and oats in large bowl; let stand 10 minutes. Stir until water is absorbed. Add granulated sugar, brown sugar and butter; beat with electric mixer at low speed 1 minute or until well blended. Beat in eggs and vanilla until well blended.

3. Add flour, cocoa and baking soda; beat until blended. Stir in 1 cup chocolate chips. Spread batter in prepared pan; sprinkle with chocolate and peanut butter chips.

4. Bake 40 minutes or until toothpick inserted into center comes out clean. Cool completely in pan on wire rack. *Makes 12 to 16 servings*

Applesauce Cake Squares

⅓ cup butter, softened

⅔ cup thawed frozen unsweetened apple juice concentrate

½ cup unsweetened applesauce

2 eggs

2 cups all-purpose flour

2 teaspoons baking powder

2 teaspoons ground cinnamon

½ teaspoon baking soda

¼ teaspoon salt

1 large apple, peeled and chopped

Cinnamon Whipped Cream (recipe follows, optional)

1. Preheat oven to 375°F. Spray 8- or 9-inch square baking pan with nonstick cooking spray.

2. Beat butter in large bowl with electric mixer until creamy. Beat in apple juice concentrate, applesauce and eggs until well blended. Add flour, baking powder, cinnamon, baking soda and salt; beat until well blended. Stir in apple. Spread batter in prepared pan.

3. Bake 20 to 25 minutes or until toothpick inserted into center comes out clean. Cool in pan on wire rack. Serve warm or at room temperature with Cinnamon Whipped Cream, if desired.   *Makes 9 servings*

Cinnamon Whipped Cream: Beat ½ cup whipping cream in medium bowl with electric mixer at high speed until soft peaks form. Add 1 teaspoon vanilla and ¼ teaspoon ground cinnamon; beat until stiff peaks form.

Pineapple Raisin Cake

- 2 eggs
- 1 cup thawed frozen unsweetened pineapple juice concentrate
- ¼ cup (½ stick) butter, melted
- 1 teaspoon vanilla
- 1⅓ cups all-purpose flour
- ⅔ cup old-fashioned oats
- 1 teaspoon baking soda
- 1 teaspoon ground cinnamon
- ½ teaspoon ground ginger
- ¼ teaspoon salt
- ⅛ teaspoon ground nutmeg
- 1 can (8 ounces) crushed pineapple, well drained
- ¾ cup lightly toasted chopped pecans
- ½ cup golden raisins

1. Preheat oven to 350°F. Spray 12×8-inch baking dish with nonstick cooking spray.

2. Beat eggs in large bowl. Add pineapple juice concentrate, butter and vanilla; beat until well blended. Add flour, oats, baking soda, cinnamon, ginger, salt and nutmeg; beat until blended. Stir in pineapple, pecans and raisins. Spread batter in prepared baking dish.

3. Bake 18 to 20 minutes or until firm. Cool completely in pan on wire rack.

Makes 12 to 16 servings

Tortoise Snack Cake

- 1 package (about 15 ounces) devil's food cake mix, plus ingredients to prepare mix
- 1 cup chopped pecans
- 1 cup semisweet chocolate chips
- ½ teaspoon vanilla
- ½ cup caramel topping

  Additional caramel topping and chopped pecans (optional)

1. Preheat oven to 350°F. Spray 13×9-inch baking pan with nonstick cooking spray.

2. Prepare cake mix according to package directions; stir in pecans, chocolate chips and vanilla. Spread batter in prepared pan. Drizzle ½ cup caramel topping over batter; swirl caramel into batter with knife.

3. Bake 30 to 35 minutes or until cake begins to pull away from sides of pan and toothpick inserted into center comes out clean. Cool slightly on wire rack. Top with additional caramel topping and pecans, if desired.

Makes 12 to 16 servings

Teatime Carrot Cake

½ cup packed brown sugar

⅓ cup butter, softened

1 egg

½ cup milk

1 teaspoon vanilla

1¼ cups all-purpose flour

¾ cup finely shredded carrots

2 teaspoons baking powder

1 teaspoon pumpkin pie spice

¼ teaspoon salt

⅓ cup raisins

Powdered sugar (optional)

1. Preheat oven to 350°F. Spray 8-inch square baking pan with nonstick cooking spray.

2. Combine sugar and butter in large bowl; beat with electric mixer at medium speed 2 minutes or until well blended. Beat in egg until light and fluffy. Add milk and vanilla; beat until well blended. Stir in flour, carrots, baking powder, pumpkin pie spice and salt just until blended. Stir in raisins. Spread batter in prepared pan.

3. Bake 30 to 35 minutes or until toothpick inserted into center comes out clean. Cool completely in pan on wire rack.

4. Sprinkle with powdered sugar just before serving, if desired.

Makes 9 servings

Margarita Cheesecake

   2 packages (8 ounces each) cream cheese, softened
   ½ cup sour cream
   ½ cup sugar
   2 eggs
   2 tablespoons tequila
   2 tablespoons orange liqueur
      Grated peel and juice of 1 lime
   1 (9-inch) graham cracker crust
  20 to 25 small pretzel sticks, crushed (optional)
      Lime slices (optional)

1. Preheat oven to 350°F.

2. Combine cream cheese, sour cream and sugar in food processor; process until very smooth. Add eggs; process until completely combined. Add tequila, liqueur, lime peel and lime juice; process until smooth. Pour batter into crust.

3. Bake 40 minutes or until center is just set. Cool about 30 minutes. Refrigerate until thoroughly chilled. (Cheesecake will firm up as it cools.)

4. Sprinkle crushed pretzels around edge of cheesecake and garnish with lime slices, if desired.   *Makes 8 servings*

Variation: Before pouring into crust, add 8 to 10 drops green food coloring; process until color is evenly distributed.

Cranberry Chocolate Cake

   1 **package (about 15 ounces) devil's food cake mix**

1⅓ **cups water**

   3 **eggs**

  ½ **cup vegetable or canola oil**

   1 **can (14 ounces) whole berry cranberry sauce, divided**

   1 **container (8 ounces) thawed frozen whipped topping**

   2 **tablespoons unsweetened cocoa powder**

   1 **cup sliced almonds, toasted***

*To toast almonds, spread in single layer on baking sheet. Bake in preheated 350°F oven 5 to 7 minutes or until golden brown, stirring occasionally.

1. Preheat oven to 350°F. Spray 13×9-inch baking pan with nonstick cooking spray.

2. Combine cake mix, water, eggs and oil in large bowl; beat 1 to 2 minutes or until well blended. Add half of cranberry sauce; beat until well blended. Spread batter in prepared pan.

3. Bake about 30 minutes or until toothpick inserted into center comes out clean. Cool completely in pan on wire rack.

4. Sift cocoa into whipped topping; stir until blended.

5. Heat remaining cranberry sauce in microwave on HIGH 15 seconds or until softened. Spread evenly over cake; top with whipped topping mixture. Sprinkle with almonds just before serving.   *Makes 12 to 16 servings*

S'More Snack Cake

  1 **package (about 15 ounces) yellow cake mix, plus ingredients to prepare mix**
  1 **cup chocolate chunks, divided**
2½ **cups bear-shaped graham crackers, divided**
1½ **cups mini marshmallows**

1. Preheat oven to 350°F. Spray 13×9-inch baking pan with nonstick cooking spray.

2. Prepare cake mix according to package directions; stir in ½ cup chocolate chunks and 1 cup graham crackers. Spread batter in prepared pan.

3. Bake 30 minutes. Remove cake from oven; sprinkle with remaining ½ cup chocolate chunks and marshmallows. Arrange remaining 1½ cups graham crackers evenly over top.

4. Bake 8 minutes or until marshmallows are golden brown. Cool completely in pan on wire rack.
Makes 12 to 16 servings

Note: This cake is best served the day it is made.

Spicy Pumpkin Pie Cake

1¾ cups all-purpose flour

1½ cups packed brown sugar

  2 teaspoons ground cinnamon

1¾ teaspoons baking powder

  1 teaspoon baking soda

  ½ teaspoon ground ginger

  ¼ teaspoon salt

  ¼ teaspoon ground cloves

  1 can (15 ounces) solid-pack pumpkin

  4 eggs

  ⅔ cup vegetable or canola oil

  1 cup raisins

    Powdered sugar (optional)

1. Preheat oven to 350°F. Spray 13×9-inch baking pan with nonstick cooking spray.

2. Combine flour, brown sugar, cinnamon, baking powder, baking soda, ginger, salt and cloves in large bowl. Add pumpkin, eggs and oil; beat with electric mixer at medium speed 2 minutes or until well blended. Stir in raisins. Spread batter in prepared pan.

3. Bake about 30 minutes or until toothpick inserted into center comes out clean. Cool completely in pan on wire rack.

4. Sprinkle with powdered sugar just before serving, if desired.

Makes 12 to 16 servings

German Upside Down Cake

1½ cups flaked coconut

1 cup chopped pecans

1 container (16 ounces) coconut pecan frosting

1 package (about 15 ounces) German chocolate cake mix

1⅓ cups water

4 eggs

1 cup milk chocolate chips

⅓ cup vegetable or canola oil

Whipped cream (optional)

1. Preheat oven to 350°F. Spray 13×9-inch glass baking dish with nonstick cooking spray.

2. Spread coconut in prepared baking dish. Sprinkle pecans over coconut. Spoon frosting by tablespoonfuls over pecans. Do not spread.

3. Combine cake mix, water, eggs, chocolate chips and oil in large bowl; beat 1 to 2 minutes or until well blended. Spread batter in prepared pan over frosting.

4. Bake 35 minutes or until toothpick inserted into center comes out clean. Cool in pan 10 minutes. Invert onto serving plate; serve warm. Top with whipped cream, if desired.   *Makes 12 to 16 servings*

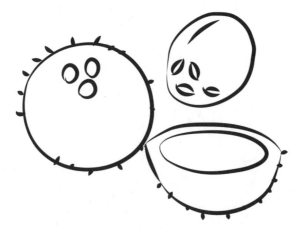

Poppy Seed Cake

2 eggs

½ cup thawed frozen unsweetened apple juice concentrate

⅓ cup butter, melted

1 tablespoon grated lemon peel

1 tablespoon lemon juice

1 teaspoon vanilla

1 cup all-purpose flour

⅓ cup poppy seeds

1½ teaspoons baking powder

½ teaspoon baking soda

⅛ teaspoon salt

1. Preheat oven to 350°F. Spray 9-inch square baking pan with nonstick cooking spray.

2. Beat eggs in large bowl. Add apple juice concentrate, butter, lemon peel, lemon juice and vanilla; beat 1 to 2 minutes or until well blended. Add flour, poppy seeds, baking powder, baking soda and salt; beat until blended. Spread batter in prepared pan.

3. Bake 20 minutes or until edges are golden brown and toothpick inserted into center comes out clean. Cool in pan on wire rack. Serve warm or at room temperature.   *Makes 9 servings*

Whole Wheat Carrot Cake

    2   cups packed brown sugar
    1¾ cups whole wheat flour
    2   teaspoons baking soda
    1   teaspoon salt
    1   teaspoon ground cinnamon
    ½   teaspoon ground nutmeg
    ¼   teaspoon ground cloves
    1   cup vegetable or canola oil
    4   eggs
    3   cups lightly packed grated carrots
    1   teaspoon vanilla
        Powdered sugar (optional)

1. Preheat oven to 350°F. Spray 8-inch square baking pan with nonstick cooking spray.

2. Combine brown sugar, flour, baking soda, salt, cinnamon, nutmeg and cloves in large bowl; mix well. Stir in oil until well blended. Beat in eggs, one at a time, until well blended. Stir in carrots and vanilla. Spread batter in prepared pan.

3. Bake 45 to 55 minutes or until top of cake springs back when lightly touched. Cool completely in pan on wire rack.

4. Sprinkle with powdered sugar just before serving, if desired.

Makes 9 servings

tip: To save time, purchase grated carrots in the produce section of the supermarket. Or grate whole peeled carrots using your food processor with the grating disk.

Crunchy Peach Snack Cake

- 1 package (9 ounces) yellow cake mix
- 1 container (6 ounces) peach yogurt
- 1 egg
- ¼ cup peach fruit spread
- ¾ cup square whole grain oat cereal with cinnamon, slightly crushed
  Whipped cream (optional)

1. Preheat oven to 350°F. Spray 8-inch square baking pan with nonstick cooking spray.

2. Combine cake mix, yogurt and egg in medium bowl; beat with electric mixer at medium speed 1 to 2 minutes or until well blended. Spread batter in prepared pan. Drop fruit spread by ½ teaspoonfuls over top. Sprinkle with cereal.

3. Bake 25 minutes or until toothpick inserted into center comes out clean. Cool completely in pan on wire rack. Serve with whipped cream, if desired.

Makes 9 servings

Double Chocolate Chip Snack Cake

  1 package (about 15 ounces) devil's food cake mix, divided
  2 eggs
½ cup water
¼ cup vegetable or canola oil
½ teaspoon ground cinnamon
  1 cup semisweet chocolate chips, divided
¼ cup packed brown sugar
  2 tablespoons butter, melted
¾ cup white chocolate chips, melted

1. Preheat oven to 350°F. Spray 10-inch round cake pan with nonstick cooking spray. Reserve ¾ cup dry cake mix.

2. Combine remaining cake mix, eggs, water, oil and cinnamon in large bowl; beat with electric mixer at medium speed 2 minutes. Spread batter in prepared pan; sprinkle with ½ cup semisweet chocolate chips.

3. Combine reserved dry cake mix and brown sugar in same bowl. Stir in butter and remaining ½ cup semisweet chocolate chips. Sprinkle over batter in pan.

4. Bake 35 minutes or until toothpick inserted into center comes out clean. Cool in pan 10 minutes; remove to wire rack to cool completely.

5. Drizzle white chocolate over cooled cake.   *Makes 8 to 10 servings*

Ginger Sweet Potato Cake

1 package (about 15 ounces) spice cake mix

1⅓ cups water

1 can (15 ounces) sweet potatoes, drained and mashed

3 eggs

2 tablespoons vegetable or canola oil

1 tablespoon grated fresh ginger

1 container (8 ounces) thawed frozen whipped topping

1. Preheat oven to 350°F. Spray 13×9-inch baking pan with nonstick cooking spray.

2. Combine cake mix, water, sweet potatoes, eggs, oil and ginger in large bowl; beat 2 minutes or until well blended. Spread batter in prepared pan.

3. Bake 30 minutes or until toothpick inserted into center comes out clean. Cool completely in pan on wire rack.

4. Spread whipped topping over cake just before serving.

Makes 12 to 16 servings

Fruit Cocktail Cake

   2 **cups all-purpose flour**

   2 **cups fruit cocktail, drained**

1¾ **cups sugar**

 ½ **cup butter (1 stick), melted**

  2 **eggs**

  2 **teaspoons baking soda**

 ½ **teaspoon salt**

1. Preheat oven to 350°F. Spray 13×9-inch baking pan with nonstick cooking spray.

2. Combine flour, fruit cocktail, sugar, butter, eggs, baking soda and salt in large bowl; mix well. Spread batter in prepared pan.

3. Bake 40 minutes or until toothpick inserted into center comes out clean. Cool completely in pan on wire rack. *Makes 12 to 16 servings*

Peanut Butter Picnic Cake

  1 **package (about 15 ounces) yellow cake mix**
1¼ **cups water**
  3 **eggs**
  1 **cup peanut butter, divided**
  1 **teaspoon vanilla**
  1 **cup powdered sugar**
  ½ **cup (1 stick) butter, softened**
  1 **tablespoon milk**
  1 **cup coarsely chopped salted dry-roasted peanuts**

1. Preheat oven to 350°F. Spray 13×9-inch baking pan with nonstick cooking spray.

2. Combine cake mix, water, eggs, ½ cup peanut butter and vanilla in large bowl; beat 1 to 2 minutes or until well blended. Spread batter in prepared pan.

3. Bake 25 to 30 minutes or until toothpick inserted into center comes out clean. Cool completely in pan on wire rack.

4. Combine powdered sugar and butter in large bowl; beat with electric mixer at medium speed until smooth and creamy. Add remaining ½ cup peanut butter and milk; beat until light and fluffy. Spread frosting over cooled cake; sprinkle with peanuts. *Makes 12 to 16 servings*

Butter Brickle Cake

1 package (about 15 ounces) yellow cake mix
1 package (4-serving size) butterscotch instant pudding and pie filling mix
4 eggs
¾ cup water
¾ cup vegetable or canola oil
1 cup chopped walnuts, divided
⅔ cup sugar, divided
2 teaspoons ground cinnamon, divided

1. Preheat oven to 350°F. Grease and flour 13×9-inch baking pan.

2. Combine cake mix, pudding mix, eggs, water and oil in large bowl; beat with electric mixer at medium speed 4 minutes or until fluffy. Spread half of batter in prepared pan. Sprinkle with ½ cup walnuts, ½ cup sugar and 1 teaspoon cinnamon. Top with remaining batter; sprinkle with remaining ½ cup walnuts, ½ cup sugar and 1 teaspoon cinnamon.

3. Bake 40 minutes or until toothpick inserted into center comes out clean. Cool completely in pan on wire rack. *Makes 12 to 16 servings*

Serving Suggestion: Serve warm with whipped cream or vanilla ice cream.

Applesauce Cake

  2 cups sugar

1½ cups applesauce

½ cup shortening

½ cup water

  2 eggs

2¾ cups all-purpose flour

1½ teaspoons baking soda

¾ teaspoon ground cinnamon

½ teaspoon ground cloves

½ teaspoon ground allspice

¼ teaspoon baking powder

  1 cup raisins

½ cup chopped walnuts

1. Preheat oven to 350°F. Spray 13×9-inch baking pan with nonstick cooking spray.

2. Combine sugar, applesauce, shortening, water and eggs in large bowl; beat 2 minutes or until well blended. Stir in flour, baking soda, cinnamon, cloves, allspice and baking powder until blended. Stir in raisins and walnuts. Spread batter in prepared pan.

3. Bake 25 to 30 minutes or until toothpick inserted into center comes out clean. Cool in pan on wire rack. Serve warm or at room temperature.

Makes 12 to 16 servings

Chocolate Yogurt Snack Cake

⅔ cup plus 2 tablespoons unsweetened Dutch process cocoa powder, divided

1¼ cups sugar

6 tablespoons (¾ stick) butter, softened

2 eggs

1¾ cups all-purpose flour

2 teaspoons baking powder

1 teaspoon salt

½ teaspoon baking soda

1 cup whole-milk plain yogurt

⅓ cup water

1 teaspoon vanilla

Quick Chocolate Frosting (recipe follows, optional)

1. Preheat oven to 350°F. Spray 13×9-inch baking pan with nonstick cooking spray. Dust with 2 tablespoons cocoa powder; tap out excess.

2. Beat sugar and butter in large bowl with electric mixer at medium speed about 1 minute or until light and fluffy. Add eggs; beat 1 minute. Gradually stir in remaining ⅔ cup cocoa, flour, baking powder, salt and baking soda; beat at low speed just until combined. Stir in 1 cup yogurt, water and vanilla; beat 1 minute or until blended. Spread batter in prepared pan.

3. Bake 35 to 40 minutes or until toothpick inserted into center comes out clean. Cool completely in pan on wire rack.

4. Prepare Quick Chocolate Frosting, if desired. Spread over cooled cake.

Makes 12 to 16 servings

Quick Chocolate Frosting: Combine 1 cup semisweet chocolate chips and 1 cup whole-milk plain yogurt in medium microwavable bowl. Microwave on HIGH 30 seconds; stir. Continue microwaving at 10-second intervals until chocolate is melted and mixture is smooth. Whisk in ½ cup powdered sugar until well blended.

Favorite Potluck Carrot Cake

1 package (about 15 ounces) yellow cake mix
1 package (4-serving size) vanilla instant pudding and pie filling mix
3 cups grated carrots
1 can (8 ounces) crushed pineapple, undrained
4 eggs
½ cup chopped walnuts
½ cup water
2 teaspoons ground cinnamon
Cream Cheese Frosting (recipe follows, optional) *or* 1 container (16 ounces) prepared cream cheese frosting

1. Preheat oven to 350°F. Spray 13×9-inch baking pan with nonstick cooking spray.

2. Combine cake mix, pudding mix, carrots, pineapple, eggs, walnuts, water and cinnamon in large bowl; beat 1 to 2 minutes or until well blended. Spread batter in prepared pan.

3. Bake 40 to 45 minutes or until toothpick inserted into center comes out clean. Cool completely in pan on wire rack.

4. Prepare Cream Cheese Frosting, if desired. Spread over cooled cake.

Makes 12 to 16 servings

Cream Cheese Frosting: Combine 2 packages (8 ounces each) softened cream cheese, ½ cup (1 stick) softened butter and 2 teaspoons vanilla in large bowl; beat with electric mixer 3 minutes or until fluffly. Gradually add 2 cups powdered sugar; beat until well blended.

Oat Apricot Snack Cake

  1 container (6 ounces) plain whole-milk yogurt
  ¾ cup packed brown sugar
  ½ cup granulated sugar
  ⅓ cup vegetable or canola oil
  1 egg
  2 tablespoons milk
  2 teaspoons vanilla
  1 cup all-purpose flour
  ½ cup whole wheat flour
  1 teaspoon baking soda
  1 teaspoon ground cinnamon
  ½ teaspoon salt
  2 cups old-fashioned oats
  1 cup chopped dried apricots (about 6 ounces)
  Glaze (recipe follows, optional)

1. Preheat oven to 350°F. Spray 13×9-inch baking pan with nonstick cooking spray.

2. Combine yogurt, brown sugar, granulated sugar, oil, egg, milk and vanilla in large bowl; mix well. Add all-purpose flour, whole wheat flour, baking soda, cinnamon and salt; stir until well blended. Stir in oats and apricots. Spread batter in prepared pan.

3. Bake 25 to 30 minutes or until toothpick inserted into center comes out clean. Cool completely in pan on wire rack.

4. Prepare Glaze, if desired. Drizzle over cooled cake.

Makes 12 to 16 servings

Glaze: Combine 1 cup powdered sugar and 2 tablespoons milk in small bowl; whisk until smooth.

NO FUSS
Bundt Cakes

Quick Triple Chocolate Cake

   1 package (about 15 ounces) chocolate cake mix
   1 package (4-serving size) chocolate instant pudding and pie filling mix
   1 cup sour cream
   4 eggs
   ½ cup water
   ½ cup vegetable or canola oil
   1 cup semisweet chocolate chips or chunks
      Powdered sugar

1. Preheat oven to 350°F. Spray 12-cup (10-inch) bundt pan with nonstick cooking spray.

2. Combine cake mix, pudding mix, sour cream, eggs, water and oil in large bowl; beat 2 minutes or until well blended. Stir in chocolate chips. Pour batter into prepared pan.

3. Bake 50 minutes or until toothpick inserted near center comes out clean. Cool in pan 10 minutes; invert onto wire rack to cool completely.

4. Sprinkle with powdered sugar just before serving.   *Makes 12 servings*

Lemon Berry Bundt

- 1 package (about 18 ounces) lemon cake mix
- 5 eggs
- 1 cup plain yogurt
- ⅓ cup vegetable or canola oil
- 1 tablespoon grated lemon peel
- 8 ounces frozen mixed berries, thawed and patted dry*
  Lemon Glaze (recipe follows, optional)

*Or substitute 1½ cups fresh berries in season; slice the strawberries, if used.

1. Preheat oven to 325°F. Spray 12-cup (10-inch) bundt pan with nonstick cooking spray.

2. Combine cake mix, eggs, yogurt, oil and lemon peel in large bowl; beat 1 to 2 minutes or until well blended. Spoon half of batter into prepared pan; sprinkle with berries. Pour remaining batter over berries.

3. Bake 50 to 55 minutes or until toothpick inserted near center comes out clean. Cool in pan on wire rack 15 minutes. Gently loosen edge and center of cake with knife; invert onto wire rack.

4. Prepare Lemon Glaze, if desired. Spoon over warm cake. Serve warm or at room temperature.   *Makes 12 servings*

Lemon Glaze: Combine 1 cup powdered sugar, 2 tablespoons melted butter, 2 tablespoons lemon juice and 1 teaspoon vanilla in small bowl; whisk until smooth.

Double Butterscotch Cake

1½ cups self-rising flour

1 cup sugar

1 cup sour cream

4 eggs

1 package (4-serving size) butterscotch instant pudding and pie filling mix

½ cup water

½ cup vegetable or canola oil

1 package (10 ounces) butterscotch chips

1. Preheat oven to 325°F. Spray 12-cup (10-inch) bundt pan with nonstick cooking spray.

2. Combine flour, sugar, sour cream, eggs, pudding mix, water and oil in large bowl; beat with electric mixer at medium speed 2 minutes or until well blended. Stir in butterscotch chips. Pour batter into prepared pan.

3. Bake 45 to 60 minutes or until toothpick inserted near center comes out clean. Cool in pan 15 minutes; invert onto wire rack to cool completely.

Makes 12 servings

Orange Rum Cake

- 3 cups all-purpose flour
- 2 cups sugar
- 2 teaspoons baking powder
- ½ teaspoon salt
- 1 cup orange juice
- 3 eggs
- ½ cup (1 stick) butter, melted
- ½ cup chopped pecans
- ½ cup golden rum, divided

1. Preheat oven to 350°F. Spray 12-cup (10-inch) bundt pan with nonstick cooking spray.

2. Combine flour, sugar, baking powder and salt in large bowl. Add orange juice, eggs and butter; beat 2 minutes or until well blended. Stir in pecans and ¼ cup rum. Pour batter into prepared pan.

3. Bake 50 to 60 minutes or until toothpick inserted near center comes out clean. Cool in pan 10 minutes. Drizzle with remaining ¼ cup rum; invert onto serving plate to cool completely.   *Makes 12 servings*

Apple Spice Cake

- 1 can (21 ounces) apple pie filling
- 1 package (about 15 ounces) spice cake mix
- 3 eggs
- 2 teaspoons ground cinnamon
- 1 cup powdered sugar
  Glaze (recipe follows, optional)

1. Preheat oven to 350°F. Grease and flour 12-cup (10-inch) bundt pan.

2. Place apple pie filling in large bowl. Cut apples into ¼-inch pieces with paring knife or scissors. Add cake mix, eggs and cinnamon; beat with electric mixer at medium speed 2 minutes or until well blended. Pour batter into prepared pan.

3. Bake 45 to 55 minutes or until toothpick inserted near center comes out clean. Cool in pan 1 hour; invert onto serving plate to cool completely.

4. Prepare Glaze, if desired. Drizzle over cooled cake.   *Makes 12 servings*

Glaze: Combine 1 cup powdered sugar, 1½ teaspoons milk and ¼ teaspoon vanilla in small bowl; whisk until smooth.

Coconut Almond Cake

- ¾ cup sliced almonds, toasted,* divided
- 1 package (about 15 ounces) yellow cake mix
- 1 package (4-serving size) vanilla instant pudding and pie filling mix
- 4 eggs
- 1 cup sour cream
- ¾ cup water
- ¼ cup vegetable or canola oil
- ½ teaspoon coconut extract
- ½ teaspoon vanilla
- ⅔ cup flaked coconut, divided
- Chocolate Glaze (recipe follows, optional)

To toast almonds, spread in single layer on baking sheet. Bake in 350°F oven 5 to 7 minutes or until golden brown, stirring frequently.

1. Preheat oven to 350°F. Spray 12-cup (10-inch) bundt pan with nonstick cooking spray. Coarsely chop ½ cup almonds.

2. Combine cake mix, pudding mix, eggs, sour cream, water, oil, coconut extract and vanilla in large bowl; beat 2 minutes or until well blended. Fold in chopped almonds and ⅓ cup coconut. Pour batter into prepared pan.

3. Bake 1 hour or until toothpick inserted near center comes out clean. Cool cake in pan 10 minutes; invert onto wire rack to cool completely.

4. Prepare Chocolate Glaze, if desired. Pour over cooled cake; sprinkle with remaining ¼ cup almonds and ⅓ cup coconut.   *Makes 12 servings*

Chocolate Glaze: Heat ½ cup whipping cream in small saucepan just until hot (do not boil). Remove from heat; add ½ cup semisweet chocolate chips and let stand 2 minutes. Whisk until smooth. Let stand at room temperature 15 to 20 minutes or until slightly thickened.

Lemon-Lime Pound Cake

- 3 cups sugar
- 1½ cups (3 sticks) butter, softened
- 5 eggs
- 2 teaspoons lemon extract
- 3 cups cake flour
- ¾ cup lemon-lime soda

1. Preheat oven to 325°F. Grease and flour 12-cup (10-inch) bundt pan.

2. Combine sugar and butter in large bowl; beat with electric mixer at medium speed 3 minutes or until light and fluffy. Beat in eggs, one at a time, beating well after each addition. Beat in lemon extract. Beat in flour and soda until blended. Pour batter into prepared pan.

3. Bake 1 hour or until toothpick inserted near center comes out clean. Cool in pan 15 minutes; invert onto wire rack to cool completely.

Makes 12 servings

Peanut Butter Cookie Cake

- 1 package (about 15 ounces) white cake mix
- 1 package (4-serving size) vanilla instant pudding and pie filling mix
- 4 eggs
- ½ cup milk
- ⅓ cup vegetable or canola oil
- ¼ cup water
- ¼ cup creamy peanut butter
- 2 cups chopped peanut butter cookies, divided
- ½ cup semisweet chocolate chips, melted

1. Preheat oven to 350°F. Spray 12-cup (10-inch) bundt pan with nonstick cooking spray.

2. Combine cake mix, pudding mix, eggs, milk, oil, water and peanut butter in large bowl; beat 2 minutes or until well blended. Stir in 1¾ cups chopped cookies. Pour batter into prepared pan.

3. Bake 50 to 60 minutes or until toothpick inserted near center comes out clean. Cool in pan 10 minutes; invert onto wire rack to cool completely.

4. Spoon melted chocolate over cake; sprinkle with remaining ¼ cup chopped cookies.

Makes 12 servings

Butterscotch Cinnamon Bundt Cake

- 1 package (about 15 ounces) yellow cake mix
- 1 package (4-serving size) butterscotch instant pudding and pie filling mix
- 1 cup water
- 3 eggs
- 2 teaspoons ground cinnamon
- ½ cup chopped pecans
  Powdered sugar (optional)

1. Preheat oven to 325°F. Spray 12-cup (10-inch) bundt pan with nonstick cooking spray.

2. Combine cake mix, pudding mix, water, eggs and cinnamon in large bowl; beat 2 minutes or until well blended. Stir in pecans. Pour batter into prepared pan.

3. Bake 40 to 50 minutes or until cake springs back when lightly touched. Cool in pan 10 minutes; invert onto serving plate to cool completely.

4. Sprinkle with powdered sugar just before serving, if desired.

Makes 12 servings

Pistachio Walnut Bundt Cake: Substitute white cake mix for yellow cake mix, pistachio pudding mix for butterscotch pudding mix and walnuts for pecans.

Light Chocolate Bundt Cake

  1 package (about 15 ounces) chocolate cake mix

  ¾ cup warm water

  3 eggs

  3 jars (2½ ounces each) puréed baby food prunes

  2 tablespoons vegetable or canola oil

  2 teaspoons instant coffee granules

     White Chocolate Glaze (recipe follows, optional)

1. Preheat oven to 350°F. Grease and flour 12-cup (10-inch) bundt pan.

2. Combine cake mix, water, eggs, prunes, oil and coffee granules in large bowl; beat 2 minutes or until well blended. Pour batter into prepared pan.

3. Bake 40 minutes or until toothpick inserted near center comes out clean. Cool in pan 10 minutes; invert onto serving plate to cool completely.

4. Prepare White Chocolate Glaze, if desired. Pour warm glaze over cooled cake. Let stand about 30 minutes.   *Makes 12 servings*

White Chocolate Glaze: Combine ½ cup white chocolate chips and 1 tablespoon milk in small microwavable bowl. Microwave on MEDIUM (50%) 50 seconds; stir. Microwave on MEDIUM at additional 30-second intervals until chips are completely melted; stir after each 30-second interval.

146 Peach Melba Cake

Blackberry Almond Cake

Simple S'More Cake

Cranberry Pear Cake

Autumn Dump Cake

Island Delight Cake

Citrus Cake

      3 cups all-purpose flour
    2¾ cups sugar
      1 teaspoon baking powder
      ¼ teaspoon salt
    1¼ cups (2½ sticks) butter, softened
      5 eggs
      ⅔ cup milk
      1 teaspoon lemon extract
      1 teaspoon orange extract
         Citrus Cream Cheese Frosting (recipe follows, optional)

1. Preheat oven to 350°F. Grease and flour 12-cup (10-inch) bundt pan.

2. Combine flour, sugar, baking powder and salt in large bowl. Add butter, eggs and milk; beat with electric mixer at medium speed 2 minutes or until well blended. Stir in extracts. Pour batter into prepared pan.

3. Bake 50 to 60 minutes or until toothpick inserted near center comes out clean. Cool in pan 15 minutes; invert onto wire rack to cool completely.

4. Prepare Citrus Cream Cheese Frosting, if desired. Spread frosting over cooled cake. Refrigerate 1 to 2 hours. *Makes 12 servings*

Citrus Cream Cheese Frosting: Combine 1 package (8 ounces) softened cream cheese, 1 container (8 ounces) thawed frozen whipped topping, ¼ cup sugar, 1 teaspoon orange extract and 1 teaspoon lemon extract in large bowl; beat with electric mixer at medium speed 2 minutes or until creamy.

Zucchini Spice Bundt Cake

1 package (about 15 ounces) spice or carrot cake mix

1 cup water

3 eggs

2 tablespoons vegetable or canola oil

1 medium zucchini, shredded

¼ cup chopped walnuts, toasted*

¾ teaspoon vanilla

Powdered Sugar Glaze (optional, recipe follows)

*To toast walnuts, spread in single layer on baking sheet. Bake in 350°F oven 5 to 7 minutes or until golden brown, stirring frequently.

1. Preheat oven to 325°F. Spray 12-cup (10-inch) bundt pan with nonstick cooking spray.

2. Combine cake mix, water, eggs and oil in large bowl; beat 2 minutes or until well blended. Stir in zucchini, walnuts and vanilla until blended. Pour batter into prepared pan.

3. Bake 40 minutes or until toothpick inserted near center comes out almost clean. Cool in pan 10 minutes; invert onto wire rack to cool completely.

4. Prepare Powdered Sugar Glaze, if desired. Drizzle over cake; let stand until set.

Makes 12 servings

Powdered Sugar Glaze: Combine ¼ cup powdered sugar and 1 to 2 teaspoons milk in small bowl; whisk until smooth.

Cookies 'n' Cream Cake

  1 package (about 15 ounces) white cake mix

  1 package (4-serving size) white chocolate instant pudding and pie filling mix

  1 cup vegetable or canola oil

  4 egg whites

  ½ cup milk

20 chocolate sandwich cookies, coarsely chopped

  ½ cup semisweet chocolate chips, melted

  4 chocolate sandwich cookies, cut into quarters

1. Preheat oven to 350°F. Spray 12-cup (10-inch) bundt pan with nonstick cooking spray.

2. Combine cake mix, pudding mix, oil, egg whites and milk in large bowl; beat 2 minutes or until well blended. Stir in chopped cookies. Spread batter in prepared pan.

3. Bake 50 to 60 minutes or until cake springs back when lightly touched. Cool in pan 1 hour; invert onto serving plate to cool completely.

4. Drizzle melted chocolate over cake; top with quartered cookies.

Makes 12 servings

Easy Apple Butter Cake

- 1 package (about 15 ounces) yellow cake mix
- 1 package (4-serving size) vanilla instant pudding and pie filling mix
- 1 cup sour cream
- 1 cup apple butter
- 4 eggs
- ½ cup apple juice
- ¼ cup vegetable oil
- 1 teaspoon ground cinnamon
- ½ teaspoon ground nutmeg
- ½ teaspoon ground cloves
- ¼ teaspoon salt
  Powdered sugar (optional)

1. Preheat oven to 375°F. Spray 12-cup (10-inch) bundt pan with nonstick cooking spray.

2. Combine cake mix, pudding mix, sour cream, apple butter, eggs, apple juice, oil, cinnamon, nutmeg, cloves and salt in large bowl; beat 2 minutes or until well blended. Pour batter into prepared pan.

3. Bake 45 to 50 minutes or until toothpick inserted near center comes out clean. Cool in pan 20 minutes. Run sharp knife along edge of pan to release cake; invert onto serving plate to cool completely.

4. Sprinkle with powdered sugar just before serving, if desired.

Makes 12 servings

Double Chocolate Bundt Cake

1 package (about 15 ounces) chocolate cake mix
1 package (4-serving size) chocolate instant pudding and pie filling mix
4 eggs, beaten
¾ cup water
¾ cup sour cream
½ cup vegetable or canola oil
1 cup semisweet chocolate chips
Powdered sugar (optional)

1. Preheat oven to 350°F. Spray 12-cup (10-inch) bundt pan with nonstick cooking spray.

2. Combine cake mix, pudding mix, eggs, water, sour cream and oil in large bowl; beat 2 minutes or until well blended. Stir in chocolate chips. Pour batter into prepared pan.

3. Bake 55 to 60 minutes or until cake springs back when lightly touched. Cool 1 hour in pan; invert onto serving plate to cool completely.

4. Sprinkle with powdered sugar just before serving, if desired.

Makes 12 servings

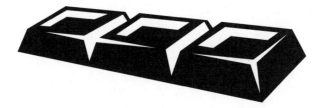

Cranberry Orange Ring

¾ cup orange juice

1 egg

2 tablespoons vegetable or canola oil

1 tablespoon grated orange peel

1 teaspoon vanilla

¼ teaspoon orange extract

2 cups all-purpose flour

1 cup sugar

1½ teaspoons baking powder

1 teaspoon salt

½ teaspoon baking soda

¼ teaspoon ground cloves

1 cup fresh or frozen cranberries

1. Preheat oven to 350°F. Spray 12-cup (10-inch) bundt pan with nonstick cooking spray.

2. Combine orange juice, egg, oil, orange peel, vanilla and orange extract in large bowl; beat 1 to 2 minutes or until well blended. Add flour, sugar, baking powder, salt, baking soda and cloves; stir just until blended. Gently fold in cranberries. Pour batter into prepared pan.

3. Bake 30 to 35 minutes (35 to 40 minutes if using frozen cranberries) or until toothpick inserted near center comes out clean. Cool in pan 15 minutes; invert onto serving plate. Serve warm or at room temperature.

Makes 12 servings

Pecan Praline Brandy Cake

  1 **package (about 15 ounces) butter pecan cake mix**

¾ **cup water**

⅓ **cup plain yogurt**

  2 **egg whites**

  1 **egg**

¼ **cup brandy**

  2 **tablespoons vegetable or canola oil**

½ **cup chopped toasted pecans***

     Praline Glaze (recipe follows, optional)

*To toast pecans, spread in single layer on baking sheet. Bake in 350°F oven 8 to 10 minutes or until lightly browned, stirring frequently.

1. Preheat oven to 350°F. Spray 12-cup (10-inch) bundt pan with nonstick cooking spray.

2. Combine cake mix, water, yogurt, egg whites, egg, ¼ cup brandy and oil in large bowl; beat with electric mixer at low speed 30 seconds. Beat at medium speed 4 minutes or until light and fluffy. Fold in ½ cup pecans. Pour batter into prepared pan.

3. Bake 50 minutes or until toothpick inserted near center comes out clean. Cool in pan 10 minutes; invert onto wire rack to cool completely.

4. Prepare Praline Glaze, if desired. Pour over cooled cake; let stand until set. *Makes 12 servings*

Praline Glaze: Combine ⅔ cup packed brown sugar, ⅓ cup corn syrup, ¼ cup whipping cream and 2 tablespoons butter in small saucepan; bring to a boil over medium heat, stirring constantly. Remove from heat; stir in ½ cup toasted chopped pecans, ½ teaspoon brandy and ½ teaspoon vanilla. Cool to room temperature.

Lemon Poppy Seed Bundt Cake

- 1 cup granulated sugar
- ½ cup (1 stick) butter, softened
- 2 eggs
- ¾ cup milk
- 2 teaspoons vanilla
- 2 cups all-purpose flour
- 2 tablespoons poppy seeds
- 1 tablespoon grated lemon peel
- 2 teaspoons baking powder
- ½ teaspoon salt
  Powdered sugar (optional)

1. Preheat oven to 350°F. Grease and flour 12-cup (10-inch) bundt pan.

2. Combine granulated sugar, butter and eggs in large bowl; beat with electric mixer at medium speed 2 minutes or until well blended. Beat in milk and vanilla until blended. Add flour, poppy seeds, lemon peel, baking powder and salt; beat 2 minutes or until smooth. Pour batter into prepared pan.

3. Bake 30 minutes or until toothpick inserted near center comes out clean. Gently loosen cake from pan with knife; invert onto wire rack to cool completely.

4. Sprinkle with powdered sugar just before serving, if desired.

Makes 12 servings

Note: One medium lemon yields about 1 tablespoon of grated lemon peel.

Mandarin Orange Tea Cake

   1   **package (16 ounces) pound cake mix**
   ½   **cup orange juice**
   2   **eggs**
   ¼   **cup milk**
   1   **can (15 ounces) mandarin orange segments, drained**
       Orange Glaze (recipe follows, optional)

1. Preheat oven to 350°F. Spray 12-cup (10-inch) bundt pan with nonstick cooking spray.

2. Combine cake mix, orange juice, eggs and milk in large bowl; beat with electric mixer at medium speed 3 minutes or until light and fluffy. Fold in orange segments. Pour batter into prepared pan.

3. Bake 45 minutes or until golden brown and toothpick inserted near center comes out clean. Cool in pan 15 minutes; invert onto wire rack to cool completely.

4. Prepare Orange Glaze, if desired. Drizzle over cooled cake; let stand until set.   *Makes 12 servings*

Orange Glaze: Combine ¾ cup powdered sugar, 2 tablespoons orange juice and grated peel of 1 orange in small bowl; whisk until smooth.

EASY
as Pie

Country Pecan Pie

  1¼ cups dark corn syrup

   4 eggs

  ½ cup packed brown sugar

  ¼ cup (½ stick) butter, melted

   2 teaspoons all-purpose flour

 1½ teaspoons vanilla

   1 unbaked deep-dish 9-inch pie crust

 1½ cups pecan halves

1. Preheat oven to 350°F.

2. Combine corn syrup, eggs, brown sugar and butter in large bowl; beat 2 minutes or until well blended. Stir in flour and vanilla until blended. Pour into crust; arrange pecans on top.

3. Bake 40 to 45 minutes or until center of filling is puffed and golden brown. Cool completely on wire rack. *Makes 8 servings*

Sour Cream Squash Pie

  1 package (14 ounces) frozen winter squash, thawed and drained

  ½ cup sour cream

  ¼ cup sugar

  1 egg

1½ teaspoons pumpkin pie spice

  ½ teaspoon salt

  ½ teaspoon vanilla

  ¾ cup evaporated milk

  1 (9-inch) graham cracker pie crust

  ¼ cup chopped hazelnuts, toasted* (optional)

*To toast hazelnuts, spread in single layer on baking sheet. Bake at 350°F 7 to 10 minutes or until lightly golden, stirring occasionally. Remove hazelnuts from pan and cool completely before chopping.

1. Preheat oven to 350°F.

2. Combine squash, sour cream, sugar, egg, pumpkin pie spice, salt and vanilla in large bowl; whisk until well blended. Whisk in evaporated milk. Pour into crust.

3. Bake 1 hour and 10 minutes or until set. Cool completely on wire rack. Sprinkle with hazelnuts just before serving, if desired.   *Makes 8 servings*

Buttermilk Pie

1½ cups sugar

1 tablespoon cornstarch

3 eggs

½ cup buttermilk

¼ cup (½ stick) butter, melted

1 tablespoon lemon juice

1 teaspoon vanilla

1 (6-ounce) graham cracker pie crust

Whipped cream (optional)

1. Preheat oven to 350°F.

2. Combine sugar and cornstarch in medium bowl. Add eggs, buttermilk, butter, lemon juice and vanilla; beat with electric mixer at medium speed 2 minutes or until smooth. Pour into crust.

3. Bake 40 minutes or until set. Cool completely on wire rack. Refrigerate 2 hours or until ready to serve. Serve with whipped cream, if desired.

Makes 8 servings

Fruit and Nut Chocolate Chip Pie

  2 eggs

½ cup packed brown sugar

¼ cup granulated sugar

  1 teaspoon vanilla

½ teaspoon grated orange peel

⅛ teaspoon salt

  1 cup (2 sticks) butter, melted

½ cup all-purpose flour

  1 cup semisweet chocolate chips

  1 cup chopped pecans or walnuts

  1 cup dried cranberries or raisins

  1 unbaked 9-inch pie crust

Whipped cream (optional)

1. Preheat oven to 325°F.

2. Combine eggs, brown sugar, granulated sugar, vanilla, orange peel and salt in large bowl; whisk until well blended. Whisk in butter and flour until blended. Stir in chocolate chips, pecans and cranberries. Pour into crust.

3. Bake 50 minutes or until top is puffed and golden brown. Cool completely on wire rack. Serve with whipped cream, if desired.   *Makes 8 servings*

Mom's Pumpkin Pie

1½ cans (15 ounces each) solid-pack pumpkin

  1 can (12 ounces) evaporated milk

  1 cup sugar

  2 eggs

  2 tablespoons maple syrup

  1 teaspoon ground cinnamon

  1 teaspoon vanilla

 ½ teaspoon salt

  2 unbaked 9-inch pie crusts

    Whipped cream (optional)

1. Preheat oven to 350°F.

2. Combine pumpkin, evaporated milk, sugar, eggs, maple syrup, cinnamon, vanilla and salt in large bowl; whisk until well blended. Pour into crusts. Place crusts on baking sheet.

3. Bake 1 hour or until knife inserted into centers comes out clean. Cool completely on wire rack. Serve with whipped cream, if desired.

Makes 16 servings

Lemon Chess Pie

  3 eggs

  2 egg yolks

1¾ cups sugar

  ½ cup half-and-half

  ⅓ cup lemon juice

  ¼ cup (½ stick) butter, melted

  3 tablespoons grated lemon peel

  2 tablespoons all-purpose flour

  1 unbaked 9-inch pie crust

     Whipped cream (optional)

1. Preheat oven to 325°F.

2. Whisk eggs and egg yolks in large bowl. Whisk in sugar, half-and-half, lemon juice, butter, lemon peel and flour until well blended. Pour into crust.

3. Bake 40 minutes or until almost set. Cool completely on wire rack. Refrigerate 2 hours or until ready to serve. Serve with whipped cream, if desired. *Makes 8 servings*

Tip: To determine doneness, carefully shake pie. It is done when only the center 2 inches jiggle.

Caribbean Coconut Pie

- 1 unbaked deep-dish 9-inch pie crust
- 1 can (14 ounces) sweetened condensed milk
- ¾ cup flaked coconut
- 2 eggs
- ½ cup hot water
- 2 teaspoons grated lime peel
  Juice of 1 lime
- ¼ teaspoon salt
- ⅛ teaspoon ground red pepper
  Whipped cream (optional)

1. Preheat oven to 400°F. Prick holes in bottom of crust with fork. Bake 10 minutes or until lightly browned. Cool 15 minutes on wire rack.

2. *Reduce oven temperature to 350°F.* Combine sweetened condensed milk, coconut, eggs, water, lime peel, lime juice, salt and red pepper in large bowl; whisk until well blended. Pour into crust.

3. Bake 30 minutes or until knife inserted into center comes out clean. Cool completely on wire rack. Serve with whipped cream, if desired.

Makes 8 servings

Bourbon Pecan Pie

¼ cup (½ stick) butter, softened

½ cup sugar

3 eggs

1½ cups light or dark corn syrup

2 tablespoons bourbon

1 teaspoon vanilla

1 unbaked deep-dish 9-inch pie crust

1 cup pecan halves

1. Preheat oven to 350°F.

2. Beat butter in large bowl with electric mixer at medium speed until creamy. Add sugar; beat 3 minutes or until fluffy. Add eggs, one at a time, beating well after each addition. Add corn syrup, bourbon and vanilla; beat until well blended. Pour filling into crust; arrange pecans on top.

3. Bake on lowest oven rack 50 to 55 minutes or until knife inserted near center comes out clean. (Filling will be puffy.) Cool completely on wire rack. Serve at room temperature or cover and refrigerate up to 24 hours.

Makes 8 servings

Raspberry Buttermilk Pie

1 unbaked deep-dish 9-inch pie crust

3 eggs, at room temperature

2 tablespoons all-purpose flour

1 cup buttermilk

¾ cup plus 2 tablespoons sugar

¼ cup (½ stick) butter, melted

¼ cup honey

½ teaspoon vanilla

¼ teaspoon salt

1½ cups fresh raspberries (do not substitute frozen)

1. Preheat oven to 425°F. Place crust on baking sheet. Bake 5 minutes. Remove from oven; press down any areas that puff up.

2. *Reduce oven temperature to 350°F.* Beat eggs and flour in large bowl until blended. Add buttermilk, sugar, butter, honey, vanilla and salt; beat until sugar is dissolved. Gently stir in raspberries. Pour into crust.

3. Bake 50 minutes or until knife inserted near center comes out clean. Check after 30 minutes; if crust browns before filling is set, lightly tent pie with foil. Let stand 30 minutes before serving. *Makes 6 servings*

Pumpkin Sweet Potato Pie

- 1 unbaked deep-dish 9-inch pie crust
- 2 cups lightly mashed cooked sweet potatoes*
- 1 can (15 ounces) solid-pack pumpkin
- 1 can (14 ounces) sweetened condensed milk
- 3 eggs
- ¼ cup (½ stick) butter, cut in small pieces
- 2 teaspoons Chinese five-spice powder
- 1½ teaspoons grated lemon peel
  Savory Whipped Cream (recipe follows, optional)

*Or substitute canned sweet potatoes.

1. Preheat oven to 350°F. Place crust on rimmed baking sheet.

2. Combine sweet potatoes, pumpkin, sweetened condensed milk, eggs, butter, five-spice powder and lemon peel in food processor; process until smooth. Pour into crust.

3. Bake about 55 minutes or until puffed and knife inserted 1 inch from center comes out clean. Cool on wire rack.

4. Prepare Savory Whipped Cream, if desired. Serve with pie.

Makes 8 servings

Savory Whipped Cream: Combine 1 cup whipping cream, 2 teaspoons grated lemon peel and ¼ teaspoon ground black pepper in medium bowl; beat with electric mixer at medium-high speed until soft peaks form. Stir in 1½ tablespoons bourbon, if desired, and 1 tablespoon lemon juice until blended.

Southern Oatmeal Pie

- 4 eggs
- 1 cup light corn syrup
- ½ cup packed brown sugar
- 6 tablespoons butter, melted and slightly cooled
- 1½ teaspoons vanilla
- ½ teaspoon salt
- 1 cup quick oats
- 1 unbaked 9-inch pie crust
- Whipped cream (optional)

1. Preheat oven to 375°F.

2. Whisk eggs in medium bowl. Add corn syrup, brown sugar, butter, vanilla and salt; whisk until well blended. Stir in oats. Pour into crust.

3. Bake 35 minutes or until edge is set. Cool on wire rack. Serve warm or at room temperature with whipped cream, if desired. *Makes 8 servings*

BREADS
& Coffeecakes

Cranberry Pumpkin Nut Bread

- 1 cup solid-pack pumpkin
- ¾ cup granulated sugar
- ½ cup packed brown sugar
- 2 eggs
- ⅓ cup vegetable or canola oil
- 2 cups all-purpose flour
- 1 tablespoon pumpkin pie spice
- 1 teaspoon baking powder
- ½ teaspoon baking soda
- ¼ teaspoon salt
- 1 cup chopped dried cranberries
- ¾ cup chopped macadamia nuts, toasted*

To toast macadamia nuts, spread in single layer on ungreased baking sheet. Bake in preheated 350°F oven 6 to 8 minutes or until lightly browned, stirring occasionally. Cool before using.

1. Preheat oven to 350°F. Spray 9×5-inch loaf pan with nonstick cooking spray.

2. Combine pumpkin, granulated sugar, brown sugar, eggs and oil in large bowl; mix well. Stir in flour, pumpkin pie spice, baking powder, baking soda and salt just until blended. Stir in cranberries and macadamia nuts. Pour batter into prepared pan.

3. Bake 45 to 50 minutes or until toothpick inserted into center comes out clean. Cool in pan 15 minutes; remove to wire rack to cool completely.

Makes 1 loaf

Blueberry Hill Bread

- ¾ cup buttermilk
- 1 egg
- ¼ cup vegetable or canola oil
- 2 cups all-purpose flour
- ¾ cup packed brown sugar
- 2 teaspoons baking powder
- 1 teaspoon baking soda
- ½ teaspoon salt
- ½ teaspoon ground nutmeg
- 1 cup fresh or thawed frozen blueberries

1. Preheat oven to 350°F. Spray 8×4-inch loaf pan with nonstick cooking spray.

2. Combine buttermilk, egg and oil in large bowl; mix well. Add flour, brown sugar, baking powder, baking soda, salt and nutmeg; stir just until blended. Gently fold in blueberries. (Batter will be stiff.) Pour batter into prepared pan.

3. Bake 50 to 60 minutes or until toothpick inserted in center comes out clean. Cool in pan 15 minutes; remove to wire rack to cool completely.

Makes 1 loaf

Spicy Gingerbread

- 2 cups all-purpose flour
- 1 cup light molasses
- ¾ cup buttermilk
- ½ cup (1 stick) butter, softened
- ½ cup packed brown sugar
- 1 teaspoon baking soda
- 1 teaspoon ground ginger
- 1 teaspoon ground cinnamon
- ¼ teaspoon salt
- ¼ teaspoon ground cloves

1. Preheat oven to 325°F. Grease and flour 9-inch square baking pan.

2. Combine flour, molasses, buttermilk, butter, brown sugar, baking soda, ginger, cinnamon, salt and cloves in large bowl; beat with electric mixer at low speed until well blended. Beat at high speed 2 minutes. Spread batter in prepared pan.

3. Bake 50 to 55 minutes or until toothpick inserted into center comes out clean. Cool in pan on wire rack about 30 minutes. Serve warm.

Makes 9 servings

Lemon Raisin Quick Bread

  1½ cups lemon yogurt

  ¼ cup (½ stick) butter, melted

  1 egg

  ½ teaspoon grated lemon peel

1¼ cups all-purpose flour

  ¾ cup whole wheat flour

  4 tablespoons sugar, divided

  2 teaspoons baking powder

  ½ teaspoon baking soda

  ¼ teaspoon salt

  1 cup raisins

  ¾ cup chopped walnuts (optional)

1. Preheat oven to 350°F. Spray 8×4-inch loaf pan with nonstick cooking spray.

2. Combine yogurt, butter, egg and lemon peel in large bowl; mix well. Add all-purpose flour, whole wheat flour, 3 tablespoons sugar, baking powder, baking soda and salt; stir just until blended. Stir in raisins and walnuts, if desired. Pour batter into prepared pan; smooth top. Sprinkle with remaining 1 tablespoon sugar.

3. Bake 40 to 45 minutes or until lightly browned and toothpick inserted into center comes out clean. Cool in pan 30 minutes; remove to wire rack to cool completely. *Makes 1 loaf*

Whole Wheat Date Nut Bread

- ¾ cup buttermilk
- ⅔ cup packed brown sugar
- 1 egg
- ¼ cup vegetable or canola oil
- 1 teaspoon grated lemon peel
- 1½ cups white whole wheat flour
- 1 teaspoon baking powder
- ½ teaspoon salt
- ¼ teaspoon baking soda
- ½ cup chopped dates
- ½ cup chopped walnuts

1. Preheat oven to 375°F. Spray 8×4-inch loaf pan with nonstick cooking spray.

2. Combine buttermilk, brown sugar, egg, oil and lemon peel in large bowl; mix well. Add flour, baking powder, salt and baking soda; stir until blended. Fold in dates and walnuts. Pour batter into prepared pan.

3. Bake 45 to 55 minutes or until toothpick inserted into center comes out clean. Cool in pan 10 minutes; remove to wire rack to cool completely.

Makes 1 loaf

Chocolate Chip Elvis Bread

- 1 cup mashed ripe bananas (about 2 large)
- 1 cup milk
- ¾ cup peanut butter
- ¼ cup vegetable or canola oil
- 1 egg
- 1 teaspoon vanilla
- 2½ cups all-purpose flour
- ½ cup granulated sugar
- ½ cup packed brown sugar
- 1 tablespoon baking powder
- ¾ teaspoon salt
- 1 cup semisweet chocolate chips

1. Preheat oven to 350°F. Spray two 8×4-inch loaf pans with nonstick cooking spray.

2. Combine bananas, milk, peanut butter, oil, egg and vanilla in large bowl; mix well. Add flour, granulated sugar, brown sugar, baking powder and salt; stir just until blended. Stir in chocolate chips. Pour batter into prepared pans.

3. Bake 50 minutes or until toothpick inserted into centers comes out clean. Cool in pans 10 minutes; remove to wire racks to cool completely.

Makes 2 loaves

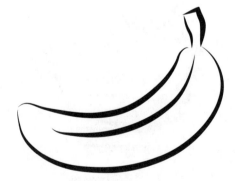

Irish Soda Bread

2½ cups all-purpose flour

1¼ cups whole wheat flour

1 cup currants

¼ cup sugar

4 teaspoons baking powder

2 teaspoons caraway seeds (optional)

1 teaspoon salt

½ teaspoon baking soda

½ cup (1 stick) butter, cut into small pieces

1⅓ to 1½ cups buttermilk

1. Preheat oven to 350°F. Line large baking sheet with parchment paper or spray with nonstick cooking spray.

2. Combine all-purpose flour, whole wheat flour, currants, sugar, baking powder, caraway seeds, if desired, salt and baking soda in large bowl.

3. Cut in butter with pastry blender or two knives until mixture resembles coarse crumbs. Add buttermilk; mix until slightly sticky dough forms. Transfer dough to prepared baking sheet; shape into 8-inch round.

4. Bake 50 to 60 minutes or until bread is golden and crust is firm. Cool on baking sheet 10 minutes; remove to wire rack to cool completely.

Makes 12 servings

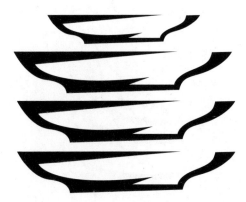

Pineapple Crunch Coffeecake

1¾ cups biscuit baking mix

½ cup plus 2 tablespoons milk

½ cup wheat germ

½ cup sour cream

¼ cup granulated sugar

1 egg

1 teaspoon vanilla

2 cans (8 ounces each) crushed pineapple, drained

⅓ cup packed dark brown sugar

⅓ cup old-fashioned or quick oats

1. Preheat oven to 350°F. Spray 8-inch square baking pan with nonstick cooking spray.

2. Combine baking mix, milk, wheat germ, sour cream, granulated sugar, egg and vanilla in large bowl; mix well. (Batter will be lumpy.) Spread batter in prepared pan. Top with pineapple; sprinkle with brown sugar and oats.

3. Bake 30 minutes or until toothpick inserted into center comes out clean. Cool in pan 10 minutes. Serve warm or at room temperature.

Makes 9 servings

Zucchini Orange Bread

  1 **package (about 17 ounces) cranberry-orange muffin mix**
1½ **cups shredded zucchini (about 6 ounces)**
  1 **cup water**
  1 **teaspoon ground cinnamon**
  1 **teaspoon grated orange peel**

1. Preheat oven to 350°F. Spray 8×4-inch loaf pan with nonstick cooking spray.

2. Combine muffin mix, zucchini, water, cinnamon and orange peel in large bowl; stir just until blended. Pour batter into prepared pan.

3. Bake 40 minutes or until toothpick inserted into center comes out almost clean. Cool in pan 5 minutes; remove to wire rack to cool completely.

Makes 1 loaf

Sweet Potato Pineapple Breakfast Bread

- 1 can (15 ounces) sweet potatoes, drained
- 2 cups all-purpose flour, divided
- 1 cup packed brown sugar
- ½ cup milk
- 2 eggs
- ⅓ cup vegetable or canola oil
- 1 tablespoon baking powder
- 1 teaspoon grated orange peel
- 1 teaspoon ground cinnamon
- ¼ teaspoon baking soda
- ¼ teaspoon salt
- 1 can (8 ounces) pineapple tidbits, drained

1. Preheat oven to 350°F. Spray 9×5-inch loaf pan with nonstick cooking spray.

2. Combine sweet potatoes, 1 cup flour, brown sugar, milk, eggs, oil, baking powder, orange peel, cinnamon, baking soda and salt in large bowl; beat with electric mixer at low speed until blended. Beat at high speed 2 minutes or until smooth. Beat in remaining 1 cup flour at low speed. Fold in pineapple. Pour batter into prepared pan.

3. Bake 55 to 60 minutes or until toothpick inserted into center comes out almost clean. Cool completely in pan on wire rack. *Makes 1 loaf*

Spiced Nut Bread

1¾ cups buttermilk

1 cup sugar

½ cup vegetable or canola oil

1 egg

1 teaspoon vanilla

½ teaspoon almond extract

3 cups all-purpose flour

1 cup chopped pecans, coarsely crushed

2 teaspoons baking powder

2 teaspoons ground cinnamon

¾ teaspoon ground nutmeg

½ teaspoon salt

¼ teaspoon ground allspice

1. Preheat oven to 350°F. Grease and flour 9×5-inch loaf pan.

2. Combine buttermilk, sugar, oil, egg, vanilla and almond extract in large bowl; mix well. Add flour, pecans, baking powder, cinnamon, nutmeg, salt and allspice; stir just until blended. (Batter will be very thick.) Pour batter into prepared pan.

3. Bake 55 minutes or until toothpick inserted into center comes out clean. Cool in pan 5 minutes; remove to wire rack to cool completely.

Makes 1 loaf

tip: Pecans can be coarsely crushed in a food processor, or place them in a resealable food storage bag and crush with a rolling pin or the bottom of a heavy skillet.

Apricot Cherry Coffeecake

- ¾ cup buttermilk
- ½ cup packed brown sugar
- ¼ cup (½ stick) butter, melted
- 1 egg
- 1½ teaspoons vanilla
- ⅓ cup chopped dried tart cherries
- ⅓ cup finely chopped dried apricots
- 1½ cups all-purpose flour
- 1 teaspoon ground cinnamon
- ½ teaspoon baking powder
- ¼ teaspoon baking soda
- ¼ teaspoon salt
- 3 tablespoons flaked coconut

1. Preheat oven to 350°F. Spray 8-inch round cake pan with nonstick cooking spray.

2. Combine buttermilk, brown sugar, butter, egg and vanilla in large bowl; mix well. Stir in cherries and apricots. Add flour, cinnamon, baking powder, baking soda and salt; stir just until blended. Spread batter in prepared pan. Sprinkle with coconut.

3. Bake 25 minutes or until toothpick inserted into center comes out clean. Cool in pan on wire rack 10 minutes. Cut into wedges. Serve warm.

Makes 8 servings

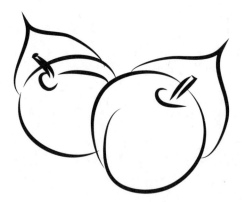

Cinnamon Apple Ring

1½ cups granulated sugar

1 cup vegetable or canola oil

2 eggs

2 teaspoons vanilla

2 medium tart apples, peeled and chopped

3 cups all-purpose flour

1 teaspoon baking soda

1 teaspoon salt

1 teaspoon ground cinnamon

1 cup chopped walnuts

Powdered sugar (optional)

1. Preheat oven to 325°F. Spray 12-cup (10-inch) bundt pan with nonstick cooking spray.

2. Combine granulated sugar, oil, eggs and vanilla in large bowl; mix well. Stir in apples. Add flour, baking soda, salt and cinnamon; stir just until blended. Stir in walnuts. Spread batter in prepared pan.

3. Bake 1 hour or until toothpick inserted near center comes out clean. Cool in pan 10 minutes. Loosen edges with metal spatula, if necessary; invert onto wire rack to cool completely.

4. Sprinkle with powdered sugar just before serving, if desired.

Makes 12 servings

Cranberry Raisin Bread

- ¾ cup milk
- 2 eggs
- 3 tablespoons butter, melted
- 1 teaspoon vanilla
- 1½ cups all-purpose flour
- ¾ cup packed brown sugar
- 1½ teaspoons baking powder
- ½ teaspoon baking soda
- ½ teaspoon ground cinnamon
- ½ teaspoon ground nutmeg
- ¼ teaspoon salt
- 1 cup coarsely chopped fresh or frozen cranberries
- ½ cup golden raisins
- ½ cup coarsely chopped pecans
- 1 tablespoon grated orange peel

1. Preheat oven to 350°F. Spray 8×4-inch loaf pan with nonstick cooking spray.

2. Combine milk, eggs, butter and vanilla in large bowl; mix well. Add flour, brown sugar, baking powder, baking soda, cinnamon, nutmeg and salt; stir just until blended. Stir in cranberries, raisins, pecans and orange peel. Pour batter into prepared pan.

3. Bake 55 to 60 minutes or until toothpick inserted into center comes out clean. Cool in pan 15 minutes; remove to wire rack to cool completely.

Makes 1 loaf

Dark Chocolate Beer Bread

½ cup (1 stick) butter, softened
½ cup packed brown sugar
1 egg
1 cup porter or other dark beer, at room temperature
1½ cups all-purpose flour
¼ cup unsweetened cocoa powder
1 teaspoon baking soda
½ teaspoon salt
¼ teaspoon white pepper
½ cup semisweet chocolate chips
½ cup chopped walnuts

1. Preheat oven to 350°F. Spray 9×5-inch loaf pan with nonstick cooking spray.

2. Combine butter and brown sugar in large bowl; beat with electric mixer at medium speed 3 minutes or until light and fluffy. Beat in egg. Add beer; beat until well blended. Add flour, cocoa, baking soda, salt and pepper; beat just until blended. Stir in chocolate chips and walnuts. Pour batter into prepared pan.

3. Bake 45 to 55 minutes or until toothpick inserted into center comes out clean. Cool in pan 10 minutes; remove to wire rack to cool completely.

Makes 1 loaf

Lemony Banana Walnut Bread

  1 cup granulated sugar
  ⅔ cup shortening
  2 eggs
1½ cups mashed ripe bananas (about 3 medium)
  6 tablespoons lemon juice
  2 cups all-purpose flour
  1 teaspoon baking soda
  1 teaspoon baking powder
  ½ teaspoon salt
  ½ cup chopped walnuts
  1 tablespoon grated lemon peel
    Lemon Glaze (recipe follows, optional)

1. Preheat oven to 325°F. Spray two 8×4-inch loaf pans with nonstick cooking spray.

2. Combine granulated sugar and shortening in large bowl; beat with electric mixer at medium speed until well blended. Add eggs, one at a time, beating well after each addition. Beat in bananas and lemon juice. Add flour, baking soda, baking powder and salt; stir just until blended. Stir in walnuts and lemon peel. Pour batter into prepared pans.

3. Bake 50 to 60 minutes or until toothpick inserted into centers comes out clean. Remove to wire racks to cool completely

4. Prepare Lemon Glaze, if desired. Drizzle over cooled loaves.

Makes 2 loaves

Lemon Glaze: Combine ½ cup powdered sugar and 1 tablespoon lemon juice in small bowl; whisk until smooth.

Ginger Pineapple Coffeecake

1¾ cups biscuit baking mix

1 container (6 ounces) vanilla yogurt

2 egg whites

¼ cup granulated sugar

2 tablespoons vegetable or canola oil

1 teaspoon grated fresh ginger

1 teaspoon vanilla

2 cans (8 ounces each) pineapple tidbits, drained

⅓ cup packed dark brown sugar

1. Preheat oven to 375°F. Spray nonstick 9-inch round cake pan or springform pan with nonstick cooking spray.

2. Combine baking mix, yogurt, egg whites, granulated sugar, oil, ginger and vanilla in large bowl; mix well. (Batter will be lumpy.) Spread batter in prepared pan. Top with pineapple; sprinkle with brown sugar.

3. Bake 25 minutes or until toothpick inserted into center comes out almost clean. Cool in pan 10 minutes. Invert cake onto plate, then invert again onto serving plate. Serve warm or at room temperature.   *Makes 9 servings*

tip: For a crunchy caramelized top, place the finished cake under the broiler for about 5 minutes or until browned.

Double Chocolate Walnut Bread

- 1½ cups milk
- 1 cup sugar
- ⅓ cup vegetable or canola oil
- 1 egg
- 1½ teaspoons vanilla
- 2¾ cups all-purpose flour
- 3 tablespoons unsweetened cocoa powder
- 2½ teaspoons baking powder
- 2 teaspoons baking soda
- 1 teaspoon salt
- ½ cup chocolate chips
- ½ cup coarsely chopped walnuts

1. Preheat oven to 350°F. Spray two 8×4-inch loaf pans with nonstick cooking spray.

2. Combine milk, sugar, oil, egg and vanilla in large bowl; mix well. Add flour, cocoa, baking powder, baking soda and salt; stir just until blended. Stir in chocolate chips and walnuts. Pour batter into prepared pans.

3. Bake 45 to 50 minutes or until toothpick inserted into centers comes out clean. Cool in pans 15 minutes; remove to wire racks to cool completely.

Makes 2 loaves

Malty Maple Corn Bread

1 cup coarse ground yellow cornmeal

1 cup porter or other dark beer

2 eggs

¼ cup (½ stick) butter, melted

¼ cup maple syrup

1 cup all-purpose flour

1 tablespoon baking powder

½ teaspoon salt

1. Preheat oven to 400°F. Spray 9-inch square baking pan with nonstick cooking spray.

2. Combine cornmeal, porter, eggs, butter and maple syrup in large bowl; mix well. Add flour, baking powder and salt; stir until well blended. Spread batter in prepared pan.

3. Bake 20 minutes or until toothpick inserted into center comes out clean. Cool in pan 10 minutes. Serve warm. *Makes 8 servings*

tip: For an extra flavorful crust, grease the baking pan with melted butter instead of cooking spray and place it in the oven for several minutes to preheat. When the batter is ready, pour it into the hot pan and bake as directed. The corn bread will develop a thick, well-browned crust.

Chocolate Chip Pumpkin Bread

     1 cup (2 sticks) butter, softened
     2 cups granulated sugar
  1½ cups solid-pack pumpkin
     4 eggs
  3½ cups all-purpose flour
     2 teaspoons baking soda
     2 teaspoons ground cinnamon
     1 teaspoon salt
     1 teaspoon ground nutmeg
     ½ teaspoon ground ginger
     ½ teaspoon ground cloves
  1½ cups semisweet chocolate chips
     1 cup chopped walnuts
        Cinnamon-Nutmeg Glaze (recipe follows, optional)

1. Preheat oven to 350°F. Spray two 9×5-inch loaf pans with nonstick cooking spray.

2. Beat butter in large bowl with electric mixer at medium speed until creamy. Add granulated sugar; beat until blended. Beat in pumpkin and eggs. Add flour, baking soda, cinnamon, salt, nutmeg, ginger and cloves; stir just until blended. Stir in chocolate chips and walnuts. Pour batter into prepared pans.

3. Bake 60 to 70 minutes or until toothpick inserted into centers comes out clean. Cool in pan 5 minutes; remove to wire rack to cool completely.

4. Prepare Cinnamon-Nutmeg Glaze, if desired. Drizzle over top of loaves.

Makes 2 loaves

Cinnamon-Nutmeg Glaze: Combine 1 cup powdered sugar, ¼ teaspoon ground cinnamon and ¼ teaspoon ground nutmeg in small bowl. Stir in 1 tablespoon milk, 1 teaspoon at a time, until smooth.

Orange Lemon Citrus Bread

- 1 **cup milk**
- ½ **cup vegetable or canola oil**
- 1 **egg**
- 1 **teaspoon vanilla**
- 1¾ **cups all-purpose flour**
- ¾ **cup sugar**
- 1 **tablespoon plus ½ teaspoon grated lemon peel, divided**
- 2 **teaspoons baking powder**
- 1½ **teaspoons grated orange peel**
- ¼ **teaspoon salt**
- ¼ **cup orange marmalade, warmed***

Microwave marmalade on HIGH 15 seconds or until slightly melted.

1. Preheat oven to 350°F. Grease and flour 9×5-inch loaf pan.

2. Combine milk, oil, egg and vanilla in large bowl; mix well. Add flour, sugar, 1 tablespoon lemon peel, baking powder, orange peel and salt; stir just until blended. (Batter will be thin.) Pour batter into prepared pan.

3. Bake 45 minutes or until toothpick inserted into center comes out clean. Cool in pan 5 minutes.

4. Meanwhile, stir remaining ½ teaspoon lemon peel into warm marmalade. Remove bread from pan to wire rack; spread marmalade mixture over top of bread. Cool completely before serving. *Makes 1 loaf*

Applesauce Spice Bread

1½ cups all-purpose flour
  1 cup unsweetened applesauce
¾ cup packed brown sugar
¼ cup shortening
  1 egg
  1 teaspoon vanilla
¾ teaspoon baking soda
¾ teaspoon ground cinnamon
¼ teaspoon baking powder
¼ teaspoon salt
¼ teaspoon ground nutmeg
½ cup toasted chopped walnuts*
½ cup raisins (optional)
    Powdered sugar

*To toast walnuts, spread in single layer on ungreased baking sheet. Bake in preheated 350°F oven 6 to 8 minutes or until lightly browned, stirring occasionally. Cool before using.

1. Preheat oven to 350°F. Spray 9-inch square baking pan with nonstick cooking spray.

2. Combine flour, applesauce, brown sugar, shortening, egg, vanilla, baking soda, cinnamon, baking powder, salt and nutmeg in large bowl; beat with electric mixer at low speed 30 seconds. Beat at high speed 3 minutes. Stir in walnuts and raisins, if desired. Spread batter in prepared pan.

3. Bake 30 minutes or until toothpick inserted into center comes out clean. Cool in pan on wire rack.

4. Sprinkle with powdered sugar just before serving. *Makes 9 servings*

Loaded Banana Bread

- **6** tablespoons (¾ stick) butter, softened
- **⅓** cup granulated sugar
- **⅓** cup packed brown sugar
- **2** eggs
- **3** ripe bananas, mashed
- **½** teaspoon vanilla
- **1½** cups all-purpose flour
- **2½** teaspoons baking powder
- **¼** teaspoon salt
- **1** can (8 ounces) crushed pineapple, drained
- **⅓** cup flaked coconut
- **¼** cup mini chocolate chips
- **⅓** cup chopped walnuts (optional)

1. Preheat oven to 350°F. Spray 9×5-inch loaf pan with nonstick cooking spray.

2. Combine butter, granulated sugar and brown sugar in large bowl; beat with electric mixer at medium speed 3 minutes or until light and fluffy. Add eggs, one at a time, beating well after each addition. Beat in bananas and vanilla. Add flour, baking powder and salt; beat just until blended. Fold in pineapple, coconut and chocolate chips. Pour batter into prepared pan. Sprinkle with walnuts, if desired.

3. Bake 50 minutes or until toothpick inserted into center comes out almost clean. Cool in pan 1 hour; remove to wire rack to cool completely.

Makes 1 loaf

Tex-Mex Quick Bread

   1 cup milk

   1 can (4 ounces) diced green chiles, drained

  ¼ cup olive oil

   1 egg

1½ cups all-purpose flour

   1 cup (4 ounces) shredded Monterey Jack cheese

  ½ cup cornmeal

  ½ cup coarsely chopped sun-dried tomatoes packed in oil

   1 can (4 ounces) sliced black olives, drained and chopped

  ¼ cup sugar

1½ teaspoons baking powder

   1 teaspoon baking soda

1. Preheat oven to 325°F. Spray 9×5-inch loaf pan with nonstick cooking spray.

2. Combine milk, chiles, oil and egg in large bowl; mix well. Add flour, cheese, cornmeal, tomatoes, olives, sugar, baking powder and baking soda; stir just until blended. Pour batter into prepared pan.

3. Bake 45 minutes or until toothpick inserted into center comes out clean. Cool in pan 15 minutes; remove to wire rack to cool completely.   *Makes 1 loaf*

Cran-Lemon Coffeecake

- 1 package (about 15 ounces) yellow cake mix
- 1 cup water
- 3 eggs
- ⅓ cup butter, melted
- ¼ cup lemon juice
- 1 tablespoon grated lemon peel
- 1½ cups coarsely chopped fresh or thawed frozen cranberries
  Lemon Glaze (recipe follows, optional)

1. Preheat oven to 350°F. Grease and flour 12-cup (10-inch) bundt pan.

2. Combine cake mix, water, eggs, butter, lemon juice and lemon peel in large bowl; beat with electric mixer at low speed 2 minutes or until well blended. Fold in cranberries. Spread batter in prepared pan.

3. Bake about 55 minutes or until toothpick inserted near center comes out clean. Cool in pan 10 minutes; invert onto wire rack.

4. Prepare Lemon Glaze, if desired. Drizzle over warm coffeecake; let stand until set. Serve warm or at room temperature. *Makes 12 servings*

Lemon Glaze: Combine 1 cup powdered sugar and 3 tablespoons lemon juice in small bowl; whisk until smooth.

Peanut Butter Mini Chip Loaves

- 1 **cup creamy peanut butter**
- ½ **cup (1 stick) butter, softened**
- ½ **cup granulated sugar**
- ½ **cup packed brown sugar**
- 2 **eggs**
- 1½ **cups buttermilk***
- 2 **teaspoons vanilla**
- 3 **cups all-purpose flour**
- 1½ **teaspoons baking powder**
- 1 **teaspoon baking soda**
- 1 **teaspoon salt**
- 1 **cup mini semisweet chocolate chips**

Or substitute soured fresh milk. To sour milk, place 1½ tablespoons lemon juice plus enough milk to equal 1½ cups in 2-cup measure. Stir; let stand 5 minutes before using.

1. Preheat oven to 350°F. Spray two 8×4-inch loaf pans with nonstick cooking spray.

2. Conbine peanut butter, butter, granulated sugar and brown sugar in large bowl; beat with electric mixer at medium speed 3 minutes or until light and fluffy. Beat in eggs, one at a time, until blended. Beat in buttermilk and vanilla. Gradually add flour, baking powder, baking soda and salt; beat at low speed just until blended. Stir in chocolate chips. Pour batter into prepared pans.

3. Bake 45 minutes or until toothpick inserted into centers comes out clean. Cool in pans 10 minutes; remove to wire rack to cool completely.

Makes 2 loaves

Spiced Pumpkin Beer Bread

1½ cups sugar

1¼ cups solid-pack pumpkin

¾ cup lager or other light-colored beer

½ cup vegetable or canola oil

2 eggs

2¼ cups all-purpose flour

2 teaspoons baking powder

1 teaspoon ground cinnamon

¾ teaspoon baking soda

½ teaspoon salt

¼ teaspoon ground nutmeg

⅛ teaspoon ground cloves

½ cup walnuts, coarsely chopped

1. Preheat oven to 350°F. Grease and flour 9×5-inch loaf pan.

2. Combine sugar, pumpkin, lager, oil and eggs in large bowl; mix well. Add flour, baking powder, cinnamon, baking soda, salt, nutmeg and cloves; stir just until blended. Fold in walnuts. Pour batter into prepared pan.

3. Bake 65 minutes or until toothpick inserted into center comes out clean. Cool in pan 10 minutes; remove to wire rack to cool completely.   *Makes 1 loaf*

Black Forest Banana Bread

  1 jar (10 ounces) maraschino cherries
  ⅔ cup packed brown sugar
  ⅓ cup butter, softened
  1 cup mashed ripe bananas (about 2 large)
  2 eggs
  1¾ cups all-purpose flour
  2 teaspoons baking powder
  ½ teaspoon salt
  1 cup semisweet chocolate chips
  ¾ cup chopped pecans

1. Preheat oven to 350°F. Spray 9×5-inch loaf pan with nonstick cooking spray. Drain cherries, reserving 2 tablespoons juice. Coarsely chop cherries.

2. Combine brown sugar and butter in large bowl; beat with electric mixer at medium speed 2 minutes or until creamy. Beat in bananas, eggs and reserved cherry juice until well blended. Add flour, baking powder and salt; stir just until blended. Stir in chopped cherries, chocolate chips and pecans Pour batter into prepared pan.

3. Bake 1 hour or until golden brown and toothpick inserted into center comes out clean. Cool in pan 10 minutes; remove to wire rack to cool completely.

Makes 1 loaf

Chocolate Cherry Coffeecake

- 2 packages (about 17 ounces each) cinnamon swirl quick bread and muffin mix
- ¾ cup chopped pecans
- 1½ cups water
- 4 eggs
- ⅓ cup vegetable or canola oil
- 1¼ cups mini semisweet chocolate chips
- 1 can (21 ounces) cherry pie filling

1. Preheat oven to 350°F. Set aside glaze packets from mixes. Generously grease and flour 12-cup (10-inch) bundt pan.

2. Sprinkle one cinnamon streusel packet and half of pecans in bottom of prepared pan. Combine quick bread mixes, water, eggs and oil in large bowl; beat 2 minutes or until well blended. Stir in chocolate chips. Spread half of batter evenly over pecans.

3. Drain cherry pie filling. (Do not rinse cherries.) Spoon cherries over batter; sprinkle with remaining packet of cinnamon streusel and pecans. Top with remaining batter.

4. Bake 45 minutes or until toothpick inserted near center comes out clean. Cool in pan 1 hour; invert onto wire rack to cool completely.

5. Prepare glaze packets according to package directions. Drizzle over cooled coffeecake; let stand until set.

Makes 12 servings

Harvest Quick Bread

    1 cup milk
    1 egg
    ¼ cup (½ stick) butter, melted
    1 cup all-purpose flour
    1 cup whole wheat flour
    ½ cup packed brown sugar
    ¼ cup granulated sugar
    1½ teaspoons baking powder
    ½ teaspoon baking soda
    ½ teaspoon salt
    ½ teaspoon ground cinnamon
    ¾ cup dried cranberries
    ½ cup chopped walnuts

1. Preheat oven to 350°F. Spray 9×5-inch loaf pan with nonstick cooking spray.

2. Combine milk, egg and butter in large bowl; mix well. Add all-purpose flour, whole wheat flour, brown sugar, granulated sugar, baking powder, baking soda, salt and cinnamon; stir just until blended. Stir in cranberries and walnuts. Pour batter into prepared pan.

3. Bake 45 to 50 minutes or until toothpick inserted into center comes out clean. Cool in pan 10 minutes; remove to wire rack to cool completely.

Makes 1 loaf

BROWNIES
& Blondies

Raspberry Brownies

- ¾ cup (1½ sticks) butter
- 2 cups sugar
- ¾ cup unsweetened cocoa powder
- 3 eggs
- 2 teaspoons vanilla
- 1 cup all-purpose flour
- 1½ cups fresh or thawed frozen raspberries

1. Line two 8-inch square baking pans with heavy-duty foil, leaving 1-inch overhang. Spray foil with nonstick cooking spray.

2. Melt butter in medium saucepan over medium heat, stirring occasionally. Remove from heat; stir in sugar and cocoa until well blended. Stir in eggs and vanilla until smooth. Stir in flour just until blended. Spread batter in prepared pans. Press raspberries gently into batter.

3. Bake 15 to 20 minutes or until centers are just set. Do not overbake. Cool completely in pans on wire racks. Lift brownies out of pans using foil; remove foil.
Makes 32 brownies

Caramel Chocolate Chunk Blondies

¾ cup granulated sugar

¾ cup packed brown sugar

½ cup (1 stick) butter, softened

2 eggs

1½ teaspoons vanilla

1½ cups all-purpose flour

1 teaspoon baking powder

½ teaspoon salt

1½ cups semisweet chocolate chunks

⅓ cup caramel topping

1. Preheat oven to 350°F. Spray 13×9-inch baking pan with nonstick cooking spray.

2. Combine granulated sugar, brown sugar and butter in large bowl; beat with electric mixer at medium speed 2 minutes or until smooth and creamy. Beat in eggs and vanilla until well blended. Add flour, baking powder and salt; beat at low speed until blended. Stir in chocolate chunks. Spread batter in prepared pan. Drop spoonfuls of caramel topping onto batter; swirl into batter with knife.

3. Bake 25 minutes or until golden brown. Cool completely in pan on wire rack. *Makes 24 blondies*

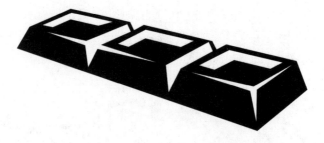

Island Brownies

2 cups sugar

4 eggs

¾ cup (1½ sticks) butter, melted

1¼ cups all-purpose flour

⅔ cup unsweetened cocoa powder

1 teaspoon baking powder

1 teaspoon salt

1 teaspoon ground ginger

¾ cup chopped macadamia nuts

¼ cup finely chopped crystallized ginger

1. Preheat oven to 350°F. Spray 13×9-inch baking pan with nonstick cooking spray.

2. Combine sugar, eggs and butter in large bowl; mix well. Add flour, cocoa, baking powder, salt and ground ginger; stir until blended. Stir in macadamia nuts and crystallized ginger. Spread batter in prepared pan.

3. Bake 25 to 30 minutes or until toothpick inserted into center comes out clean. Cool completely in pan on wire rack. *Makes 24 brownies*

Chocolate Chip Brownies

¾ cup granulated sugar

½ cup (1 stick) butter

2 tablespoons water

2 cups semisweet chocolate chips, divided

1½ teaspoons vanilla

2 eggs

1¼ cups all-purpose flour

½ teaspoon baking soda

½ teaspoon salt

   Powdered sugar (optional)

1. Preheat oven to 350°F. Spray 9-inch square baking pan with nonstick cooking spray.

2. Combine granulated sugar, butter and water in medium microwavable bowl; microwave on HIGH 1½ to 2 minutes or until butter is melted. Stir in 1 cup chocolate chips; stir until chips are melted and mixture is well blended. Stir in vanilla; let stand 5 minutes to cool.

3. Add eggs, one at a time, beating well after each addition. Add flour, baking soda and salt; stir until blended. Stir in remaining 1 cup chocolate chips. Spread batter in prepared pan.

4. Bake 25 minutes for fudgy brownies or 30 minutes for cakelike brownies. Cool completely in pan on wire rack.

5. Sprinkle with powdered sugar just before serving, if desired.

Makes 16 brownies

Primo Pumpkin Brownies

- ¾ cup packed brown sugar
- ½ cup (1 stick) butter, softened
- 1 teaspoon vanilla
- 1 egg
- 1⅓ cups all-purpose flour
- 1 cup solid-pack pumpkin
- 2 teaspoons pumpkin pie spice*
- 1 teaspoon baking powder
- ¼ teaspoon salt
- ½ cup toffee baking bits
- White Chocolate Cream Cheese Frosting (recipe follows, optional)

Or substitute 1 teaspoon ground cinnamon, ½ teaspoon ground ginger and ¼ teaspoon each ground allspice and ground nutmeg for 2 teaspoons pumpkin pie spice.

1. Preheat oven to 350°F. Spray 8-inch square baking pan with nonstick cooking spray.

2. Combine brown sugar, butter and vanilla in large bowl; beat with electric mixer at medium speed 2 minutes or until creamy. Add egg; beat until fluffy. Stir in flour, pumpkin, pumpkin pie spice, baking powder and salt until blended. Fold in toffee bits. Spread batter in prepared pan.

3. Bake 40 to 45 minutes or until toothpick inserted into center comes out clean. Cool completely in pan on wire rack.

4. Prepare White Chocolate Cream Cheese Frosting, if desired. Spread over brownies. *Makes 16 brownies*

White Chocolate Cream Cheese Frosting: Heat 2 tablespoons whipping cream in small saucepan over medium heat. Add 4 ounces chopped white chocolate; stir until completely melted. Cool slightly. Beat 6 ounces softened cream cheese and ⅓ cup powdered sugar in large bowl with electric mixer at medium speed 1 minute or until fluffy. Beat in white chocolate mixture until smooth.

Mocha Cinnamon Blondies

1¾ cups sugar

1 cup (2 sticks) butter, melted

4 eggs

1 cup all-purpose flour

2 teaspoons instant coffee granules

1 teaspoon ground cinnamon

¼ teaspoon salt

1 cup chopped pecans

¾ cup semisweet chocolate chips

1. Preheat oven to 350°F. Spray 13×9-inch baking pan with nonstick cooking spray.

2. Combine sugar, butter and eggs in large bowl; beat with electric mixer at medium speed 3 minutes or until light and fluffy. Add flour, coffee granules, cinnamon and salt; beat at low speed until blended. Stir in pecans and chocolate chips. Spread batter in prepared pan.

3. Bake 30 minutes or until edges begin to pull away from sides of pan. Cool completely in pan on wire rack. *Makes 24 blondies*

Fruit and Pecan Brownies

- 1 cup sugar
- ½ cup (1 stick) butter, softened
- 2 eggs
- 2 squares (1 ounce each) unsweetened chocolate, melted
- 1 teaspoon vanilla
- ½ cup all-purpose flour
- 1 cup chopped dried mixed fruit
- 1 cup coarsely chopped pecans, divided
- 1 cup (6 ounces) semisweet chocolate chips, divided

1. Preheat oven to 350°F. Spray 8-inch square baking pan with nonstick cooking spray.

2. Combine sugar and butter in large bowl; beat with electric mixer at medium speed 3 minutes or until light and fluffy. Add eggs, one at a time, beating well after each addition. Beat in melted chocolate and vanilla. Stir in flour, dried fruit, ½ cup pecans and ½ cup chocolate chips. Spread batter in prepared pan; sprinkle with remaining ½ cup pecans and ½ cup chocolate chips.

3. Bake 25 to 30 minutes or just until center feels firm. Cool completely in pan on wire rack.   *Makes 16 brownies*

Honey Brownies

- 1 cup (6 ounces) semisweet chocolate chips
- 6 tablespoons butter
- 2 eggs
- ⅓ cup honey
- 1 teaspoon vanilla
- ½ cup all-purpose flour
- ½ teaspoon baking powder
- Dash salt
- 1 cup chopped walnuts

1. Preheat oven to 350°F. Spray 8-inch square baking pan with nonstick cooking spray.

2. Melt chocolate chips and butter in medium heavy saucepan over low heat. Remove from heat; cool slightly. Stir in eggs, honey and vanilla. Add flour, baking powder, salt and walnuts; stir just until blended. Spread batter in prepared pan.

3. Bake 20 to 25 minutes or just until center springs back when lightly touched. Cool completely in pan on wire rack. *Makes 16 brownies*

White Chocolate Chunk Brownies

 2 eggs
1¼ cups sugar
 4 squares (1 ounce each) unsweetened chocolate, melted
 ½ cup (1 stick) butter, melted
 1 teaspoon vanilla
 ½ cup all-purpose flour
 ½ teaspoon salt
 6 squares (1 ounce each) white chocolate, cut into ¼-inch pieces
 ½ cup coarsely chopped walnuts (optional)
    Powdered sugar (optional)

1. Preheat oven to 350°F. Spray 8-inch square baking pan with nonstick cooking spray.

2. Beat eggs in large bowl with electric mixer at medium speed 30 seconds. Gradually add sugar, beating at medium speed 4 minutes or until very thick and lemon colored. Beat in melted chocolate, butter and vanilla until blended. Add flour and salt; beat at low speed just until blended. Stir in white chocolate and walnuts, if desired. Spread batter in prepared pan.

3. Bake 30 minutes or until edges just begin to pull away from sides of pan and center is set. Cool completely in pan on wire rack.

4. Sprinkle with powdered sugar just before serving, if desired.

Makes 16 brownies

Mint Chip Brownies

- ¾ cup sugar
- ½ cup (1 stick) butter
- 2 tablespoons water
- 1 cup semisweet chocolate chips or mini semisweet chocolate chips
- 1½ teaspoons vanilla
- 2 eggs
- 1¼ cups all-purpose flour
- ½ teaspoon baking soda
- ½ teaspoon salt
- 1 cup mint chocolate chips

1. Preheat oven to 350°F. Spray 9-inch square baking pan with nonstick cooking spray.

2. Combine sugar, butter and water in large microwavable bowl; microwave on HIGH 2½ to 3 minutes or until butter is melted. Stir in semisweet chips; stir gently until chips are melted and mixture is well blended. Stir in vanilla; let stand 5 minutes to cool.

3. Add eggs, one at a time, beating well after each addition. Add flour, baking soda and salt; stir until blended. Stir in mint chocolate chips. Spread batter in prepared pan.

4. Bake 25 minutes for fudgy brownies or 30 minutes for cakelike brownies. Cool completely in pan on wire rack. *Makes 16 brownies*

Red Velvet Brownies

1 package (about 15 ounces) red velvet cake mix

¾ cup (1½ sticks) butter, softened

2 eggs

1½ cup chopped pecans, divided

1 container (16 ounces) prepared cream cheese frosting

Red sprinkles (optional)

1. Preheat oven 350°F. Line 13×9-inch baking pan with foil, leaving 1-inch overhang. Spray foil with nonstick cooking spray.

2. Combine cake mix, butter and eggs in large bowl; beat with electric mixer at medium speed 1 minute. (Mixture will be thick.) Add 1 cup pecans; beat 15 seconds or just until combined. Pour batter into prepared pan. Spray fingertips with cooking spray; gently spread batter in pan.

3. Bake 25 minutes or until toothpick inserted into center comes out almost clean. Cool completely in pan on wire rack.

4. Spread frosting over brownies; sprinkle with remaining ½ cup pecans and sprinkles, if desired. Refrigerate at least 2 hours before serving.

Makes 24 brownies

Raspberry Fudge Brownies

    1 **cup sugar**

    2 **eggs**

    1 **teaspoon vanilla**

    ½ **cup (1 stick) butter, melted**

    3 **squares (1 ounce each) bittersweet chocolate,* melted**

    ¾ **cup all-purpose flour**

    ¼ **teaspoon baking powder**

    ¼ **teaspoon salt**

    ½ **cup sliced or slivered almonds**

    ½ **cup raspberry preserves**

    1 **cup milk chocolate chips**

*Or substitute one square of unsweetened chocolate plus two squares of semisweet chocolate for the bittersweet chocolate.

1. Preheat oven to 350°F. Grease and flour 8-inch square baking pan.

2. Combine sugar, eggs and vanilla in large bowl; beat until well blended. Beat in butter and melted chocolate. Add flour, baking powder and salt; stir just until blended. Spread three-fourths of batter in prepared pan; sprinkle with almonds.

3. Bake 10 minutes. Remove from oven; spread preserves over almonds. Carefully spoon remaining batter over preserves, smoothing top. Bake 25 to 30 minutes or until center is firm to the touch.

4. Immediately sprinkle chocolate chips over top. Let stand 1 to 2 minutes or until chips melt; spread evenly over brownies. Cool completely in pan on wire rack.   *Makes 16 brownies*

Peanut Butter Chip Brownies

   1 cup packed brown sugar

   ½ cup granulated sugar

   ½ cup (1 stick) butter, melted

   2 eggs

   1 cup all-purpose flour

   ⅓ cup unsweetened Dutch process cocoa powder

   ½ teaspoon baking powder

   ½ teaspoon salt

   1 cup peanut butter chips

   ½ cup chopped peanuts

1. Preheat oven to 350°F. Spray 8-inch square baking pan with nonstick cooking spray.

2. Combine brown sugar, granulated sugar and butter in large bowl; mix well. Add eggs, one at a time, beating well after each addition. Add flour, cocoa, baking powder and salt; stir just until blended. Stir in peanut butter chips and peanuts. Spread batter in prepared pan.

3. Bake 30 to 35 minutes or until edges begin to pull away from sides of pan. Cool completely in pan on wire rack. *Makes 16 brownies*

Irish Brownies

> 4 squares (1 ounce each) semisweet baking chocolate, coarsely chopped
>
> ½ cup (1 stick) butter
>
> ½ cup sugar
>
> 2 eggs
>
> ¼ cup Irish cream liqueur
>
> 1 cup all-purpose flour
>
> ½ teaspoon baking powder
>
> ¼ teaspoon salt
>
> Irish Cream Frosting (recipe follows, optional)

1. Preheat oven to 350°F. Spray 8-inch square baking pan with nonstick cooking spray.

2. Melt chocolate and butter in medium heavy saucepan over low heat, stirring constantly. Remove from heat; stir in sugar until blended. Add eggs, one at a time, beating well after each addition. Stir in liqueur. Add flour, baking powder and salt; stir just until blended. Spread batter in prepared pan.

3. Bake 22 to 25 minutes or until center is set. Remove pan to wire rack; cool completely.

4. Prepare Irish Cream Frosting, if desired. Spread over cooled brownies. Refrigerate at least 1 hour or until frosting is set.   *Makes 16 brownies*

Irish Cream Frosting: Beat 2 ounces softened cream cheese and 2 tablespoons softened butter in medium bowl with electric mixer at medium speed until smooth. Beat in 2 tablespoons Irish cream liqueur. Gradually beat in 1½ cups powdered sugar until smooth.

Orange Cappuccino Brownies

    ¾ cup (1½ sticks) butter
    2 squares (1 ounce each) semisweet chocolate, coarsely chopped
    2 squares (1 ounce each) unsweetened chocolate, coarsely chopped
  1¾ cups sugar
    1 tablespoon instant espresso powder or instant coffee granules
    3 eggs
    ¼ cup orange-flavored liqueur
    2 teaspoons grated orange peel
    1 cup all-purpose flour
       Chocolate Glaze (recipe follows, optional)

1. Preheat oven to 350°F. Spray 13×9-inch baking pan with nonstick cooking spray.

2. Melt butter and chocolate in large heavy saucepan over low heat, stirring constantly. Remove from heat; stir in sugar and espresso powder until blended. Add eggs, one at a time, beating well after each addition. Stir in liqueur and orange peel. Add flour; stir just until blended. Spread batter in prepared pan.

3. Bake 25 to 30 minutes or until center is firm to the touch. Remove pan to wire rack.

4. Prepare Chocolate Glaze, if desired. Immediately spread over warm brownies. Cool completely in pan on wire rack.   *Makes 24 brownies*

Chocolate Glaze: Combine 1 package (12 ounces) semisweet chocolate chips and 2 tablespoons butter in small microwavable bowl. Microwave on HIGH 1 minute; stir. Microwave at 30-second intervals until chocolate is melted and mixture is smooth.

Decadent Blonde Brownies

- ¾ cup granulated sugar
- ¾ cup packed brown sugar
- ½ cup (1 stick) butter, softened
- 2 eggs
- 2 teaspoons vanilla
- 1½ cups all-purpose flour
- 1 teaspoon baking powder
- ½ teaspoon salt
- 1 package (10 ounces) semisweet chocolate chunks*
- ¾ cup coarsely chopped macadamia nuts

If chocolate chunks are not available, cut 1 (10-ounce) thick chocolate candy bar into ¼-inch pieces to measure 1½ cups.

1. Preheat oven to 350°F. Spray 13×9-inch baking pan with nonstick cooking spray.

2. Combine granulated sugar, brown sugar and butter in large bowl; beat with electric mixer at medium speed 3 minutes or until light and fluffy. Beat in eggs and vanilla until blended. Add flour, baking powder and salt; beat at low speed until well blended. Stir in chocolate chunks and macadamia nuts. Spread batter in prepared pan.

3. Bake 25 to 30 minutes or until golden brown. Cool completely in pan on wire rack.

Makes 24 brownies

Cinnamon Wheat Brownies

- ½ cup (1 stick) butter, softened
- 1 cup packed dark brown sugar
- 2 eggs
- 2 squares (1 ounce each) unsweetened chocolate, melted
- 1 teaspoon ground cinnamon
- 1 teaspoon vanilla
- ¼ teaspoon baking powder
- ¼ teaspoon ground ginger
- ⅛ teaspoon ground cloves
- 1 cup coarsely chopped walnuts
- ½ cup whole wheat flour

1. Preheat oven to 350°F. Spray 8-inch square baking pan with nonstick cooking spray.

2. Combine butter, brown sugar, eggs and melted chocolate in large bowl; beat with electric mixer at medium speed 2 minutes or until creamy. Add cinnamon, vanilla, baking powder, ginger and cloves; beat until well blended. Stir in walnuts and flour until blended. Spread batter in prepared pan.

3. Bake 25 minutes or until top feels firm and dry. Cool completely in pan on wire rack.

Makes 16 brownies

Peppermint Brownies

- 2 cups sugar
- 4 eggs
- ½ cup (1 stick) butter, melted
- 4 squares (1 ounce each) unsweetened chocolate, melted
- ½ teaspoon peppermint extract
- 1 cup all-purpose flour
- 1 cup coarsely chopped walnuts (optional)
- ½ cup finely crushed peppermint candies (18 candies)*

To crush, place unwrapped candy in heavy-duty resealable food storage bag. Loosely seal bag; crush candy with rolling pin, meat mallet or heavy skillet.

1. Preheat oven to 325°F. Spray 9-inch square baking pan with nonstick cooking spray.

2. Combine sugar and eggs in large bowl; whisk until blended. Add butter, chocolate and peppermint extract; mix well. Gradually stir in flour just until blended. Stir in walnuts, if desired. Spread batter in prepared pan.

3. Bake 35 to 40 minutes or until edges begin to pull away from sides of pan. Immediately sprinkle with crushed candy. Cool completely in pan on wire rack. *Makes 16 brownies*

Tip: For more cakelike brownies, use an 8-inch square baking pan.

Chocolate Chip Sour Cream Brownies

½ cup (1 stick) butter, softened

1 cup packed brown sugar

1 cup sour cream

1 egg

1 teaspoon vanilla

½ cup unsweetened cocoa powder

½ teaspoon baking soda

¼ teaspoon salt

2 cups all-purpose flour

1 cup semisweet chocolate chips

Powdered sugar (optional)

1. Preheat oven to 350°F. Spray 13×9-inch baking pan with nonstick cooking spray.

2. Combine butter and brown sugar in large bowl; beat with electric mixer at medium speed 2 minutes or until creamy. Add sour cream, egg and vanilla; beat until light. Add cocoa, baking soda and salt; beat until smooth. Stir in flour until well blended. Stir in chocolate chips. Spread batter in prepared pan.

3. Bake 25 to 30 minutes or until center springs back when touched. Cool completely in pan on wire rack. Sprinkle with powdered sugar, if desired.

Makes 24 brownies

S'More Brownies

1 package (about 20 ounces) brownie mix

2 eggs

½ cup vegetable or canola oil

¼ cup water

1 jar (7½ ounces) marshmallow creme

12 whole graham crackers

1. Preheat oven to 350°F. Spray 13×9-inch baking pan with nonstick cooking spray.

2. Combine brownie mix, eggs, oil and water in large bowl; mix well. Spread batter in prepared pan.

3. Bake 25 minutes or until set in center. Cool in pan 10 minutes. Spread marshmallow creme evenly over brownies. Let stand 5 minutes.

4. Break graham crackers in half to form squares. Place layer of graham crackers over marshmallow layer. Cut around graham cracker squares. Carefully remove brownies from pan. Place graham cracker square underneath each brownie; press to adhere. Cool completely.

Makes 12 brownies

Aztec Brownies

   1 **cup sugar**

   3 **eggs**

   1 **tablespoon instant coffee granules**

   1 **tablespoon vanilla**

   1 **package (12 ounces) semisweet chocolate chips, melted**

   1 **cup (2 sticks) butter, melted**

   ¾ **cup all-purpose flour**

   2 **teaspoons baking powder**

   1 **teaspoon ground cinnamon**

   1 **to 2 teaspoons chili powder**

   ½ **teaspoon salt**

   ¾ **cup sliced almonds**

1. Preheat oven to 350°F. Line 13×9-inch baking pan with foil, leaving 1-inch overhang. Spray foil with nonstick cooking spray.

2. Combine sugar, eggs, coffee granules and vanilla in medium bowl; beat until well blended. Stir in melted chocolate and butter; mix well. Add flour, baking powder, cinnamon, chili powder and salt; stir until blended. Spread batter in prepared pan.

3. Bake 15 minutes. Sprinkle with almonds. Bake 20 minutes or until top is no longer shiny and toothpick inserted into center comes out almost clean. Do not overbake. Cool completely in pan on wire rack.   *Makes 24 brownies*

Tip: For easier cutting, refrigerate cooled brownies for several hours until firm and well chilled.

Fudgy Brownie Bars

1 package (about 20 ounces) brownie mix

2 eggs

⅓ cup water

⅓ cup vegetable or canola oil

1 cup semisweet chocolate chips

⅔ cup butterscotch chips*

⅔ cup chopped pecans

¾ cup flaked coconut

1 can (14 ounces) sweetened condensed milk

*Or substitute peanut butter chips.

1. Preheat oven to 350°F. Spray 13×9-inch baking pan with nonstick cooking spray.

2. Combine brownie mix, eggs, water and oil in large bowl; beat with electric mixer at medium speed 1 to 2 minutes or until well blended. Spread batter in prepared pan.

3. Bake 18 minutes. Top with chocolate chips, butterscotch chips, pecans and coconut. Pour condensed milk over top. Bake 22 to 25 minutes or until light golden brown. Cool completely in pan on wire rack. *Makes 24 brownies*

White Chocolate Almond Brownies

12 ounces white chocolate, broken into pieces

1 cup (2 sticks) butter

3 eggs

¾ cup all-purpose flour

1 teaspoon vanilla

½ cup slivered almonds

1. Preheat oven to 325°F. Grease and flour 9-inch square baking pan.

2. Melt white chocolate and butter in large heavy saucepan over low heat, stirring constantly. (White chocolate may separate.) Add eggs; beat 1 to 2 minutes or until smooth. Stir in flour and vanilla until blended. Spread batter in prepared pan. Sprinkle with almonds.

3. Bake 30 minutes or until set. Cool completely in pan on wire rack.

Makes 16 brownies

Whole Wheat Brownies

½ cup (1 stick) butter

1 cup packed brown sugar

½ cup unsweetened cocoa powder

½ cup whole wheat flour

½ teaspoon baking soda

¼ teaspoon salt

2 eggs

½ cup semisweet chocolate chips

1 teaspoon vanilla

1. Preheat oven to 350°F. Spray 8-inch square baking pan with nonstick cooking spray.

2. Melt butter in large saucepan over low heat. Add brown sugar; cook and stir about 4 minutes or until sugar is completely dissolved and mixture is smooth. Remove pan from heat; stir in cocoa until smooth. Add flour, baking soda and salt; stir until blended. Beat in eggs, one at a time. Stir in chocolate chips and vanilla. Spread batter in prepared pan.

3. Bake 15 to 20 minutes or until toothpick inserted into center comes out almost clean.
Makes 16 brownies

Rocky Road Brownies

½ cup (1 stick) butter

½ cup unsweetened cocoa powder

1 cup sugar

½ cup all-purpose flour

¼ cup buttermilk

1 egg

1 teaspoon vanilla

1 cup mini marshmallows

1 cup coarsely chopped walnuts

1 cup semisweet chocolate chips

1. Preheat oven to 350°F. Spray 8-inch square baking pan with nonstick cooking spray.

2. Heat butter and cocoa in medium saucepan over low heat until butter is melted, stirring constantly. Remove from heat; stir in sugar, flour, buttermilk, egg and vanilla until blended. Spread batter in prepared pan.

3. Bake 25 minutes or until center feels dry. Sprinkle with marshmallows, walnuts and chocolate chips. Bake 3 to 5 minutes or just until marshmallows and chocolate are slightly melted. Cool in pan on wire rack.

Makes 16 brownies

Coconut Blondies

¾ cup (1½ sticks) butter, melted

2 eggs

1 teaspoon vanilla

1⅔ cups packed brown sugar

1 cup chopped toasted pecans*

¾ cup flaked coconut

2 cups all-purpose flour

1½ tablespoons baking powder

½ teaspoon salt

*To toast pecans, spread in single layer on baking sheet. Bake in preheated 350°F oven 8 to 10 minutes or until golden brown, stirring frequently. Cool before using.

1. Preheat oven to 350°F. Spray 13×9-inch baking pan with nonstick cooking spray.

2. Combine butter, eggs and vanilla in large bowl; mix well. Add brown sugar, pecans and coconut; stir until well blended. Add flour, baking powder and salt; stir just until blended. Spread batter in prepared pan.

3. Bake 25 minutes or until toothpick inserted into center comes out clean. Cool completely in pan on wire rack. *Makes 24 blondies*

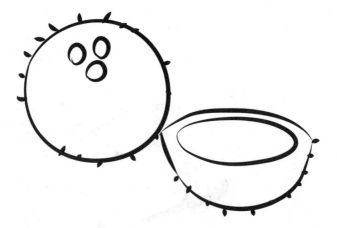

Secret Ingredient Brownies

- 1 **cup packed brown sugar**
- 1 **cup applesauce**
- ½ **cup (1 stick) butter, melted**
- 2 **eggs**
- 1 **teaspoon vanilla**
- 1 **cup all-purpose flour**
- ⅓ **cup unsweetened cocoa powder**
- ⅓ **cup mini chocolate chips**
- 2 **teaspoons baking powder**
- 2 **teaspoons baking soda**
- ½ **teaspoon salt**
- ½ **teaspoon ground cinnamon**
- **Powdered sugar (optional)**

1. Preheat oven to 350°F. Spray 8-inch square baking pan with nonstick cooking spray.

2. Combine brown sugar, applesauce, butter, eggs and vanilla in large bowl; mix well. Add flour, cocoa, chocolate chips, baking powder, baking soda, salt and cinnamon; stir until well blended. Spread batter in prepared pan.

3. Bake 30 to 35 minutes or until edges begin to pull away from sides of pan and toothpick insterted into center comes out clean. Cool completely in pan on wire rack.

4. Sprinkle with powdered sugar just before serving, if desired.

Makes 16 brownies

Mocha Fudge Brownies

¾ cup sugar

½ cup (1 stick) butter, softened

2 eggs

3 squares (1 ounce each) semisweet chocolate, melted

2 teaspoons instant espresso powder

1 teaspoon vanilla

½ cup all-purpose flour

½ cup chopped toasted almonds

1 cup milk chocolate chips, divided

1. Preheat oven to 350°F. Spray 8-inch square baking pan with nonstick cooking spray.

2. Combine sugar and butter in large bowl; beat with electric mixer at medium speed 3 minutes or until light and fluffy. Add eggs, one at a time, beating well after each addition. Add melted chocolate, espresso powder and vanilla; beat until blended. Stir in flour, almonds and ½ cup chocolate chips. Spread batter in prepared pan.

3. Bake 25 minutes or until set. Sprinkle with remaining ½ cup chocolate chips. Let stand until melted; spread evenly over brownies. Cool completely in pan on wire rack. *Makes 16 brownies*

Nutty Chocolate Cherry Brownies

  1 **cup (2 sticks) butter, cut into small chunks**

  2 **bars (3½ ounces each) semisweet chocolate, broken into pieces**

1¾ **cups sugar**

  1 **teaspoon vanilla**

  4 **eggs**

  1 **cup all-purpose flour**

 ¼ **teaspoon salt**

  1 **cup coarsely chopped walnuts, toasted***

  1 **cup dried cherries, divided**

*To toast walnuts, spread in single layer on baking sheet. Bake in preheated 350°F oven 8 to 10 minutes or until lightly browned, stirring frequently. Cool before using.

1. Preheat oven to 350°F. Spray 13×9-inch baking pan with nonstick cooking spray.

2. Melt butter and chocolate in large heavy saucepan over low heat, stirring constantly. Remove from heat; stir in sugar until blended. Stir in vanilla. Add eggs, one at a time, beating well after each addition. Add flour and salt; stir just until blended. Stir in walnuts and dried cherries. Spread batter in prepared pan.

3. Bake 32 to 35 minutes or until edges begin to pull away from sides of pan. Cool completely in pan on wire rack. *Makes 24 brownies*

Decadent Brownies

½ **cup dark corn syrup**

½ **cup (1 stick) butter**

6 **squares (1 ounce each) semisweet chocolate**

¾ **cup sugar**

3 **eggs**

1 **cup all-purpose flour**

1 **cup chopped walnuts**

1 **teaspoon vanilla**

Fudgy Glaze (recipe follows, optional)

1. Preheat oven to 350°F. Spray 8-inch square baking pan with nonstick cooking spray.

2. Combine corn syrup, butter and chocolate in large heavy saucepan over low heat; stir until chocolate is melted and mixture is smooth. Remove from heat; stir in sugar until well blended. Add eggs, flour, walnuts and vanilla; stir until blended. Spread batter in prepared pan.

3. Bake 20 to 25 minutes or just until center is set. Do not overbake.

4. Meanwhile, prepare Fudge Glaze, if desired. Spread over hot brownies immediately after removing brownies from oven. Cool completely in pan on wire rack. *Makes 16 brownies*

Fudgy Glaze: Combine 3 ounces semisweet chocolate, 2 tablespoons dark corn syrup and 1 tablespoon butter in small heavy saucepan; stir over low heat until chocolate is melted. Stir in 1 teaspoon light cream or milk.

ONE-BOWL
Bars

Banana Oatmeal Snack Bars

  2 packages (16 ounces each) refrigerated oatmeal raisin cookie dough
  2 bananas, mashed
  3 eggs
  ½ teaspoon ground cinnamon
  1 cup old-fashioned oats
  1 cup dried cranberries
  ½ cup chopped dried apricots
  ½ cup chopped pecans
     Powdered sugar (optional)

1. Preheat oven to 350°F. Let dough stand at room temperature 15 minutes. Spray 13×9-inch baking pan with nonstick cooking spray.

2. Combine dough, bananas, eggs and cinnamon in large bowl; beat 1 to 2 minutes or until well blended. Add oats, cranberries, apricots and pecans; stir until well blended. Spread dough in prepared pan.

3. Bake 40 to 45 minutes or until top is browned and center is firm to the touch. Cool completely in pan on wire rack.

4. Sprinkle with powdered sugar just before serving, if desired.

Makes 24 bars

Spicy Peach Bars

¾ cup orange juice

½ cup packed brown sugar

2 jars (2½ ounces each) baby food peaches (about ½ cup)

¼ cup vegetable or canola oil

1 egg

1 egg white

1½ cups all-purpose flour

2 teaspoons baking powder

1 teaspoon ground allspice

¾ teaspoon ground cinnamon

¼ teaspoon salt

½ cup chopped pecans

⅓ cup finely chopped dried peaches

Powdered sugar (optional)

1. Preheat oven to 350°F. Spray 13×9-inch baking pan with nonstick cooking spray.

2. Combine orange juice, brown sugar, baby food peaches, oil, egg and egg white in large bowl; beat until well blended. Add flour, baking powder, allspice, cinnamon and salt; beat just until blended. Stir in pecans and dried peaches. Pour batter into prepared pan.

3. Bake 25 to 30 minutes or until toothpick inserted into center comes out clean. Cool completely in pan on wire rack.

4. Sprinkle with powdered sugar just before serving, if desired.

Makes 24 bars

PB&J Cookie Bars

- 1 package (about 15 ounces) yellow cake mix
- 1 cup peanut butter
- ½ cup vegetable or canola oil
- 2 eggs
- 1 cup strawberry jam, warmed*
- 1 cup peanut butter chips

*Microwave jam on HIGH 20 seconds or until softened and spreadable.

1. Preheat oven to 350°F. Line 15×10-inch jelly-roll pan with foil; spray foil with nonstick cooking spray.

2. Combine cake mix, peanut butter, oil and eggs in large bowl; beat with electric mixer at medium speed 2 minutes or until well blended. With damp hands, press mixture into prepared pan.

3. Bake 20 minutes; cool 5 minutes on wire rack. Spread jam evenly over cookie crust; sprinkle with peanut butter chips.

4. Bake 10 minutes or until edges are browned. Cool completely in pan on wire rack.

Makes 40 bars

Espresso Walnut Bars

- 1 package (about 15 ounce) chocolate fudge cake mix
- 5 tablespoons butter, melted
- 2 eggs
- 2 teaspoons espresso powder or instant coffee granules
- 1 package (12 ounces) mini semisweet chocolate chips, divided
- 2 cups chopped walnuts, divided
  Espresso Glaze (recipe follows, optional)

1. Preheat oven to 350°F. Line 13×9-inch baking pan with foil; spray foil with nonstick cooking spray.

2. Combine cake mix, butter, eggs and espresso powder in large bowl; beat with electric mixer at medium speed 2 minutes or until well blended. Stir in 1 cup chocolate chips and 1 cup walnuts. Spread batter in prepared pan.

3. Bake 25 minutes or until toothpick inserted into center comes out clean. Sprinkle with remaining 1 cup chocolate chips. Let stand 5 minutes or until melted; spread chocolate evenly over bars. Sprinkle with remaining 1 cup walnuts. Cool completely in pan on wire rack.

4. Prepare Espresso Glaze, if desired. Drizzle over cooled bars.

Makes 24 bars

Espresso Glaze: Combine 1 cup powdered sugar, 1 to 2 tablespoons hot water and 2 teaspoons espresso powder or instant coffee granules in small bowl; whisk until espresso powder has dissolved and mixture is smooth.

Hawaiian Bars

10 tablespoons (1¼ sticks) butter, cubed

1 teaspoon vanilla

2 eggs

1 cup packed dark brown sugar

⅓ cup granulated sugar

1⅓ cups all-purpose flour

1 teaspoon baking powder

¼ teaspoon baking soda

¼ teaspoon salt

¾ cup coarsely chopped salted macadamia nuts

¾ cup flaked coconut

1. Preheat oven to 350°F. Spray 9-inch square baking pan with nonstick cooking spray.

2. Melt butter in large heavy saucepan over low heat. Remove from heat; stir in vanilla. Beat in eggs, one at a time. Beat in brown sugar and granulated sugar until well blended. Add flour, baking powder, baking soda and salt; stir until blended. Stir in macadamia nuts and coconut. Spread batter in prepared pan.

3. Bake 30 minutes or until edges begin to pull away from sides of pan. Cool completely in pan on wire rack.

Makes 16 bars

Note: Bars firm up and taste better on the second day.

Chocolate Cookie Magic Bars

1¾ cup chocolate cookie crumbs

½ cup (1 stick) butter, melted

1 can (14 ounces) sweetened condensed milk

1 cup semisweet chocolate chips

1 cup white chocolate chips

1 cup flaked coconut

1 cup chopped pecans

1. Preheat oven to 350°F.

2. Combine butter and cookie crumbs in medium bowl; mix well. Press crumb mixture firmly into 13×9-inch baking pan. Pour sweetened condensed milk evenly over cookie crumbs. Sprinkle with chocolate chips, coconut and pecans; press down firmly.

3. Bake 20 to 25 minutes or until lightly browned and bubbling around edges of pan. Cool completely in pan on wire rack. *Makes 24 bars*

tip: To make chocolate cookie crumbs, place plain chocolate cookies in a food processor and process until finely ground.

Door County Bars

- 10 tablespoons butter, cut into small chunks
- 1 teaspoon vanilla
- 2 eggs
- 1⅓ cups packed dark brown sugar
- 1⅓ cups all-purpose flour
- 1 teaspoon baking powder
- ¼ teaspoon baking soda
- ¼ teaspoon salt
- ½ cup diced dried apples
- ½ cup dried cherries
- ½ cup coarsely chopped toasted walnuts*

*To toast walnuts, spread in a single layer on ungreased baking sheet. Bake in 350°F oven 6 to 8 minutes or until fragrant, stirring occasionally. Cool before using.

1. Preheat oven to 350°F. Spray 9-inch square baking pan with nonstick cooking spray.

2. Melt butter in large heavy saucepan over low heat. Remove from heat; stir in vanilla. Beat in eggs, one at a time. Beat in brown sugar until well blended. Add flour, baking powder, baking soda and salt; beat until blended. Stir in apples, cherries and walnuts. Spread batter in prepared pan.

3. Bake 28 to 30 minutes or until edges begin to pull away from sides of pan. Cool completely in pan on wire rack.   *Makes 16 bars*

Oatmeal Coconut Chip Bars

- 14 tablespoons (1¾ sticks) butter, melted
- ½ cup packed brown sugar
- ¼ cup granulated sugar
- 2 eggs
- 1 teaspoon vanilla
- 1½ cups all-purpose flour
- ½ teaspoon baking powder
- ½ teaspoon salt
- 1½ cups oats
- 1½ cups semisweet chocolate chips
- ¾ cup flaked coconut

1. Preheat oven to 350°F. Spray 13×9-inch baking pan with nonstick cooking spray.

2. Combine butter, brown sugar and granulated sugar in large bowl; mix well. Beat in eggs and vanilla until well blended. Add flour, baking powder and salt; stir until blended. Stir in oats, chocolate chips and coconut. Spread batter in prepared pan.

3. Bake 20 to 25 minutes or until edges are lightly browned and center is almost set. Cool completely in pan on wire rack. *Makes 24 bars*

Easy Layered Bars

- ½ cup (1 stick) butter, melted
- 1½ cups graham cracker crumbs
- 1 can (14 ounces) sweetened condensed milk
- ½ cup coconut
- 1 cup peanut butter chips
- 1¼ cups crisp rice cereal
- 1 cup semisweet chocolate chips
- ½ cup candy-coated chocolate candies

1. Preheat oven to 340°F. Spray 13×9-inch baking pan with nonstick cooking spray.

2. Pour butter into pan. Sprinkle graham cracker crumbs evenly over butter. Pour condensed milk over crumbs. Sprinkle with coconut, peanut butter chips, cereal, chocolate chips and candies; press down gently on candies.

3. Bake 25 to 30 minutes or until top just begins to brown. Cool completely in pan on wire rack.

Makes 24 bars

S'More Bars

  1 package (16 ounces) refrigerated chocolate chip cookie dough
  ¼ cup graham cracker crumbs
  3 cups mini marshmallows
  ½ cup semisweet or milk chocolate chips
  2 teaspoons shortening

1. Preheat oven to 350°F. Spray 13×9-inch baking pan with nonstick cooking spray.

2. Press dough into prepared pan; sprinkle with graham cracker crumbs.

3. Bake 10 to 12 minutes or until edges are golden brown. Sprinkle with marshmallows; bake 2 to 3 minutes or until marshmallows are puffed. Cool completely in pan on wire rack.

4. Combine chocolate chips and shortening in small resealable food storage bag; seal bag. Microwave on HIGH 1 to 1½ minutes, kneading bag every 30 seconds until melted and smooth. Cut off small corner of bag; drizzle chocolate mixture over bars. Refrigerate 5 to 10 minutes or until chocolate is set.   *Makes 24 bars*

Tangy Lemonade Bars

- ½ cup (1 stick) butter, softened
- 1 cup sugar
- ⅓ cup thawed frozen lemonade concentrate
- 1 egg
- 2¼ cups all-purpose flour
- 1 tablespoon grated lemon peel
- ¾ teaspoon baking soda
- ¾ teaspoon salt
- 1 cup dried cranberries

1. Preheat oven to 375°F. Spray 13×9-inch baking pan with nonstick cooking spray.

2. Combine butter and sugar in large bowl; beat with electric mixer at medium speed 2 minutes or until creamy. Beat in lemonade concentrate and egg until blended. (Mixture may appear curdled.) Add flour, lemon peel, baking soda and salt; beat just until blended. Stir in cranberries. Press dough into prepared pan.

3. Bake 20 to 25 minutes or until golden brown. Cool completely in pan on wire rack.

Makes 24 bars

Butterscotch Bars

½ cup butterscotch ice cream topping

½ cup packed brown sugar

1 egg

¼ cup (½ stick) butter, melted

1 teaspoon vanilla

¾ cup all-purpose flour

½ cup chopped pecans, toasted*

¼ teaspoon salt

*To toast pecans, spread in a single layer on ungreased baking sheet. Bake in preheated 350°F oven 6 to 8 minutes or until fragrant, stirring occasionally. Cool before using.

1. Preheat oven to 350°F. Spray 8-inch square baking pan with nonstick cooking spray.

2. Combine butterscotch topping, brown sugar, egg, butter and vanilla in large bowl; mix well. Add flour, pecans and salt; stir until blended. Spread batter in prepared pan.

3. Bake 15 to 18 minutes or until firm. Cool completely in pan on wire rack.

Makes 16 bars

tip: These sweet bars are the perfect packable treat. Wrap individually in plastic wrap so they will be ready to grab for the lunch box.

Raspberry Coconut Bars

1⅔ cups graham cracker crumbs

½ cup (1 stick) butter, melted

2⅔ cups (7 ounces) flaked coconut

1 can (14 ounces) sweetened condensed milk

1 cup raspberry jam

⅓ cup finely chopped nuts

½ cup semisweet chocolate chips, melted

¼ cup white chocolate chips, melted

1. Preheat oven to 350°F. Spray 13×9-inch baking pan with nonstick cooking spray.

2. Combine graham cracker crumbs and butter in medium bowl; mix well. Spread in prepared pan; sprinkle with coconut. Pour condensed milk over coconut.

3. Bake 20 to 25 minutes or until firm and lightly browned. Cool completely in pan on wire rack. Spread jam over coconut; refrigerate 3 hours. Sprinkle with nuts; drizzle with semisweet and white chocolate. *Makes 24 bars*

Cappuccino Crunch Bars

- 1½ cups packed brown sugar
- 1 cup (2 sticks) butter, softened
- ½ cup granulated sugar
- 2 eggs
- 2 teaspoons instant coffee granules or espresso powder, dissolved in 1 tablespoon hot water
- 2 teaspoons vanilla
- 1 teaspoon grated orange peel (optional)
- 1¾ cups all-purpose flour, sifted
- 1 teaspoon baking soda
- 1 teaspoon salt
- ½ teaspoon ground cinnamon
- 1 cup white chocolate chips
- 1 cup chocolate-covered toffee baking bits

1. Preheat oven to 350°F. Spray 13×9-inch baking pan with nonstick cooking spray.

2. Combine brown sugar, butter and granulated sugar in large bowl; beat with electric mixer at medium speed 3 minutes or until fluffy. Add eggs, one at a time, beating well after each addition. Add coffee mixture, vanilla and orange peel, if desired; beat until well blended. Add flour, baking soda, salt and cinnamon; stir just until blended. Stir in white chocolate chips and toffee bits. Spread batter in prepared pan.

3. Bake 25 to 35 minutes or until golden brown and center is firm to the touch. Cool completely in pan on wire rack.   *Makes 24 bars*

Chocolate Chip Shortbread

½ cup (1 stick) butter, softened

½ cup sugar

1 teaspoon vanilla

1 cup all-purpose flour

¼ teaspoon salt

½ cup mini semisweet chocolate chips

1. Preheat oven to 375°F.

2. Combine butter and sugar in large bowl; beat with electric mixer at medium speed 3 minutes or until light and fluffy. Beat in vanilla. Add flour and salt; beat just until blended. Stir in chocolate chips. Divide dough in half; press each half into ungreased 8-inch round cake pan.

3. Bake 12 minutes or until edges are golden brown. Score shortbread with knife (8 triangles per pan), taking care not to cut completely through shortbread.

4. Cool in pans 10 minutes; remove to wire racks to cool completely. Break into triangles. *Makes 16 triangles*

Oat Toffee Bars

- ¾ cup (1½ sticks), softened
- 1 package (about 15 ounces) yellow cake mix
- 2 cups quick oats
- ¼ cup packed brown sugar
- 1 egg
- ½ teaspoon vanilla
- 1 cup toffee baking bits
- ½ cup chopped pecans
- ⅓ cup semisweet chocolate chips, melted

1. Preheat oven to 350°F. Spray 13×9-inch baking pan with nonstick cooking spray.

2. Beat butter in large bowl with electric mixer at medium speed 2 minutes or until creamy. Add cake mix, oats, brown sugar, egg and vanilla; beat until well blended. Stir in toffee bits and pecans. Press dough into prepared pan.

3. Bake 30 to 35 minutes or until golden brown. Cool completely in pan on wire rack. Drizzle melted chocolate over bars; let stand until set.

Makes 24 bars

Applesauce Fudge Bars

    1 cup packed brown sugar
    ⅔ cup unsweetened applesauce
    2 eggs
    1 teaspoon vanilla
    1 cup all-purpose flour
    ½ teaspoon baking powder
    ¼ teaspoon baking soda
    ½ cup (1 stick) butter, melted
    3 squares (1 ounce each) semisweet chocolate, melted
    ½ cup walnuts, chopped
    1 cup milk chocolate chips

1. Preheat oven to 350°F. Spray 9-inch square baking pan with nonstick cooking spray.

2. Combine brown sugar, applesauce, eggs and vanilla in large bowl; mix well. Add flour, baking powder and baking soda; beat until blended. Stir in butter and melted chocolate until blended. Spread batter in prepared pan; sprinkle with nuts.

3. Bake 25 to 30 minutes or just until set. Sprinkle with chocolate chips. Let stand 3 minutes or until melted; spread chocolate evenly over bars. Cool completely in pan on wire rack.   *Makes about 3 dozen bars*

Classic Layer Bars

- 1½ cups graham cracker crumbs
- ½ cup (1 stick) butter, melted
- 1⅓ cups flaked coconut
- 1½ cups semisweet chocolate chips or chunks*
- 1 cup chopped nuts
- 1 can (14 ounces) sweetened condensed milk

*Or substitute white chocolate, butterscotch or peanut butter chips for the chocolate chips.

1. Preheat oven to 350°F. Spray 13×9-inch baking pan with nonstick cooking spray.

2. Combine graham cracker crumbs and butter in medium bowl; press firmly into prepared pan. Sprinkle with coconut, chocolate chips and nuts; press down firmly. Pour sweetened condensed milk evenly over top.

3. Bake 25 to 30 minutes or until golden brown. Cool completely in pan on wire rack.   *Makes 24 bars*

Note: Bake at 325°F if using a glass baking dish.

Apricot Bars

- 2 eggs
- 1 cup apricot fruit spread
- ½ cup (1 stick) butter, melted
- 2 teaspoons vanilla
- 1 cup all-purpose flour
- ⅔ cup old-fashioned oats
- 1¼ teaspoons baking powder
- ¾ teaspoon ground cinnamon
- ¼ teaspoon salt
- ¼ teaspoon ground allspice
- ⅛ teaspoon ground mace

1. Preheat oven to 350°F. Spray 12×8-inch baking dish with nonstick cooking spray.

2. Beat eggs in large bowl. Beat in fruit spread, butter and vanilla until well blended. Add flour, oats, baking powder, cinnamon, salt, allspice and mace; stir until blended. Spread dough in prepared baking dish.

3. Bake 18 minutes or until golden brown and firm to the touch. Cool completely in dish on wire rack. *Makes 24 bars*

Trail Mix Breakfast Bars

- **1** package (about 15 ounces) spice cake mix
- **½** cup old-fashioned oats
- **½** cup (1 stick) butter, melted
- **2** eggs
- **2** tablespoons packed brown sugar
- **2** packages (6 ounces each) trail mix *or* ⅔ cup *each* candy-coated chocolate pieces, chopped nuts and raisins

1. Preheat oven to 350°F. Line 13×9-inch baking pan with foil; spray foil with nonstick cooking spray.

2. Combine cake mix, oats, butter, eggs and brown sugar in large bowl; beat with electric mixer at medium speed 2 minutes or until well blended. Stir in trail mix. With damp hands, press mixture into prepared pan.

3. Bake 25 minutes or until edges are lightly browned. Cool completely in pan on wire rack.   *Makes 24 bars*

Chocolate Butterscotch Bars

1½ cups packed brown sugar

1 cup (2 sticks) butter, softened

2 eggs

2¼ cups all-purpose flour

2 teaspoons baking powder

½ teaspoon salt

½ cup semisweet chocolate chips

½ cup butterscotch chips

¼ cup milk chocolate chips

1. Preheat oven to 350°F. Spray 15×10-inch jelly-roll pan with nonstick cooking spray.

2. Combine brown sugar and butter in large bowl; beat with electric mixer at medium speed 3 minutes or until light and fluffy. Add eggs; beat until well blended. Add flour, baking powder and salt; stir just until blended. Stir in semisweet chips, butterscotch chips and milk chocolate chips. Spread batter in prepared pan.

3. Bake 25 to 30 minutes or until edges are lightly browned and toothpick inserted into center comes out clean. Cool completely in pan on wire rack.

Makes 40 bars

Piña Colada Cookie Bars

½ cup (1 stick) butter, melted

1½ cups graham cracker crumbs

1 can (14 ounces) sweetened condensed milk

2 tablespoons dark rum

2 cups white chocolate chips

1 cup flaked coconut

½ cup chopped macadamia nuts

½ cup chopped dried pineapple

1. Preheat oven to 350°F.

2. Pour butter into 13×9-inch baking pan, tilting pan to coat bottom. Sprinkle with graham cracker crumbs. Combine sweetened condensed milk and rum in medium bowl; mix well. Pour over graham cracker crumbs; top with white chips, coconut, macadamia nuts and pineapple.

3. Bake 25 minutes or until edges are lightly browned. Cool completely in pan on wire rack.

Makes 24 bars

Chocolate Chunk Oat Bars

   1 cup packed brown sugar
   ½ cup (1 stick) butter, softened
   1 egg
   1 tablespoon water
   1 teaspoon vanilla
 1½ cups old-fashioned oats
   1 cup all-purpose flour
   ½ teaspoon baking soda
   ½ teaspoon salt
   2 cups semisweet chocolate chunks, divided

1. Preheat oven to 375°F. Spray 9-inch square baking pan with nonstick cooking spray.

2. Combine brown sugar and butter in large bowl; beat with electric mixer at medium-high speed 2 minutes or until creamy. Add egg, water and vanilla; beat until well blended. Add oats, flour, baking soda and salt; stir until blended. Stir in 1½ cups chocolate chunks. Spread dough in prepared pan; sprinkle with remaining ½ cup chocolate chunks.

3. Bake 25 to 30 minutes or just until center feels firm. Cool completely in pan on wire rack. *Makes 16 bars*

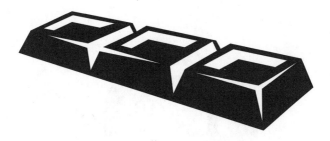

Peanut Butter Candy Bars

- 1 cup packed brown sugar
- ¾ cup crunchy peanut butter
- ½ cup granulated sugar
- ½ cup (1 stick) butter, softened
- 2 eggs
- 1 teaspoon vanilla
- ¼ cup milk
- 1¾ cups all-purpose flour
- 1 teaspoon baking powder
- 1 package (10 ounces) candy-coated peanut butter candies (1⅓ cups), divided
- ⅓ cup coarsely chopped peanuts
- 1 container (16 ounces) chocolate frosting

1. Preheat oven to 325°F. Spray 13×9-inch baking pan with nonstick cooking spray.

2. Combine brown sugar, peanut butter, granulated sugar and butter in large bowl; beat with electric mixer at medium speed 2 minutes or until creamy. Add eggs and vanilla; beat until fluffy. Gradually beat in milk. Gradually add flour and baking powder; beat until well blended. Stir in 1 cup candies and peanuts. Spread batter in prepared pan.

3. Bake 40 to 45 minutes or until toothpick inserted into center comes out clean. Cool completely in pan on wire rack. Spread frosting over bars; sprinkle with remaining ⅓ cup candies.   *Makes 24 bars*

Black Forest Bars

  1 **package (about 15 ounces) dark chocolate cake mix**

 ½ **cup (1 stick) butter, melted**

  1 **egg**

 ½ **teaspoon almond extract**

1¼ **cups sliced almonds, divided**

  1 **jar (about 16 ounces) maraschino cherries, well drained**

 ½ **cup semisweet chocolate chips**

1. Preheat oven to 350°F. Line 13×9-inch baking pan with foil, leaving 1-inch overhang.

2. Combine cake mix, butter, egg and almond extract in large bowl; beat with electric mixer at medium speed 2 minutes or until well blended. Stir in ¾ cup almonds. Press dough into prepared pan; sprinkle with cherries.

3. Bake 20 to 25 minutes or until toothpick inserted into center comes out clean. Cool completely in pan on wire rack.

4. Place chocolate chips in small resealable food storage bag; seal bag. Microwave on HIGH 1 to 1½ minutes, kneading bag every 30 seconds until melted and smooth. Cut off small corner of bag; drizzle chocolate over bars. Sprinkle with remaining ½ cup almonds. *Makes 24 bars*

Easy Turtle Bars

1 package (about 15 ounces) chocolate cake mix

½ cup (1 stick) butter, melted

¼ cup milk

1 cup (6 ounces) semisweet chocolate chips

1 cup chopped pecans, divided

1 jar (12 ounces) caramel topping

1. Preheat oven to 350°F. Spray 13×9-inch baking pan with nonstick cooking spray.

2. Combine cake mix, butter and milk in large bowl; mix well. Spread half of batter in prepared pan.

3. Bake 8 minutes or until crust begins to form. Sprinkle chocolate chips and ½ cup pecans over crust. Drizzle with caramel topping. Drop spoonfuls of remaining batter onto caramel; sprinkle with remaining ½ cup pecans. Bake 18 minutes or until top springs back when lightly touched. (Caramel center will be soft.) Cool completely in pan on wire rack. *Makes 24 bars*

No-Fuss Bar Cookies

- **2** cups chocolate cookie crumbs
- **1** cup (6 ounces) semisweet chocolate chips
- **1** cup flaked coconut
- **¾** cup coarsely chopped walnuts
- **1** can (14 ounces) sweetened condensed milk

1. Preheat oven to 350°F. Spray 13×9-inch baking pan with nonstick cooking spray.

2. Combine cookie crumbs, chocolate chips, coconut and walnuts in medium bowl; mix well. Add condensed milk; stir with spoon until well blended. Spread batter in prepared pan.

3. Bake 15 to 18 minutes or until edges are golden brown. Cool completely in pan on wire rack.

Makes 24 bars

Oat Nut Bars

½ cup (1 stick) butter

½ cup honey

¼ cup packed brown sugar

¼ cup corn syrup

2¾ cups quick oats

⅔ cup raisins

½ cup salted peanuts

1. Preheat oven to 300°F. Spray 9-inch square baking pan with nonstick cooking spray.

2. Melt butter, honey, brown sugar and corn syrup in medium saucepan over medium heat, stirring constantly. Bring to a boil; boil 8 minutes or until mixture thickens slightly. Stir in oats, raisins and peanuts until well blended. Press mixture into prepared pan.

3. Bake 25 to 30 minutes or until golden brown. Score into 2-inch squares. Cool completely in pan on wire rack. Cut into bars along score lines.

Makes 16 bars

Apricot Shortbread Diamonds

1 package (about 15 ounces) yellow cake mix

2 eggs

¼ cup vegetable or canola oil

1 tablespoon water

1 cup apricot jam or orange marmalade*

1 cup diced dried apricots (about 6 ounces)

1 cup sliced almonds

Microwave jam on HIGH 20 seconds or until softened and spreadable.

1. Preheat oven to 350°F. Line 15×10-inch jelly-roll pan with foil; spray foil with nonstick cooking spray.

2. Combine cake mix, eggs, oil and water in large bowl; beat with electric mixer at medium speed 2 minutes or until well blended. With damp hands, press mixture into prepared pan. Spread jam over dough; sprinkle with apricots and almonds.

3. Bake 25 minutes or until edges are browned and jam is bubbly at edges. Cool completely in pan on wire rack. To cut cookies into diamonds, cut crosswise at 2-inch intervals, then cut diagonally at 2-inch intervals.

Makes 40 bars

Cinnamon Apple Pie Bars

   1 package (about 15 ounces) spice cake mix
   2 cups old-fashioned oats
   ½ teaspoon ground cinnamon
   ¾ cup (1½ sticks) butter, cut into pieces
   1 egg
   1 can (21 ounces) apple pie filling

1. Preheat oven to 350°F. Spray 13×9-inch baking pan with nonstick cooking spray.

2. Combine cake mix, oats and cinnamon in large bowl. Cut in butter with pastry blender or two knives until mixture resembles coarse crumbs. Stir in egg until well blended.

3. Press three fourths of oat mixture into prepared pan. Spread apple pie filling over top. Crumble remaining oat mixture over filling.

4. Bake 25 to 30 minutes or until lightly browned. Cool completely in pan on wire rack.   *Makes 24 bars*

Mystical Layered Bars

- ⅓ cup butter
- 1 cup graham cracker crumbs
- ½ cup old-fashioned or quick oats
- 1 can (14 ounces) sweetened condensed milk
- 1 cup flaked coconut
- ¾ cup semisweet chocolate chips
- ¾ cup dried cranberries
- 1 cup coarsely chopped pecans

1. Preheat oven to 350°F. Melt butter in 13×9-inch baking pan. Remove from oven.

2. Sprinkle graham cracker crumbs and oats over butter; press down with fork. Pour condensed milk evenly over oats. Top with coconut, chocolate chips, cranberries and pecans.

3. Bake 25 to 30 minutes or until lightly browned. Cool in pan 5 minutes; cut into bars. Cool completely in pan on wire rack. *Makes 24 bars*

Peanut Butter Cookie Bars

  1 **package (16 ounces) refrigerated peanut butter cookie dough**
  1 **can (14 ounces) sweetened condensed milk**
 ¼ **cup all-purpose flour**
 ¼ **cup peanut butter**
  1 **cup peanut butter chips**
  1 **cup chopped peanuts**

1. Preheat oven to 350°F. Spray 13×9-inch baking pan with nonstick cooking spray. Let dough stand at room temperature 15 minutes.

2. Press dough into prepared pan. Bake 10 minutes.

3. Meanwhile, combine sweetened condensed milk, flour and peanut butter in large bowl; beat until well blended. Spoon over partially baked crust. Sprinkle with peanut butter chips and peanuts; press down lightly.

4. Bake 15 to 18 minutes or until center is set. Cool completely in pan on wire rack. *Makes 24 bars*

Mississippi Mud Bars

- ¾ cup packed brown sugar
- ½ cup (1 stick) butter, softened
- 1 egg
- 1 teaspoon vanilla
- ½ teaspoon baking soda
- ¼ teaspoon salt
- 1 cup plus 2 tablespoons all-purpose flour
- 1 cup (6 ounces) semisweet chocolate chips, divided
- 1 cup (6 ounces) white chocolate chips, divided
- ½ cup chopped walnuts or pecans

1. Preheat oven to 375°F. Line 9-inch square baking pan with foil; spray foil with nonstick cooking spray.

2. Combine brown sugar and butter in large bowl; beat with electric mixer at medium speed 2 minutes or until creamy. Beat in egg and vanilla until well blended. Beat in baking soda and salt. Add flour; stir until blended. Stir in ⅔ cup semisweet chips, ⅔ cup white chips and walnuts. Spread batter in prepared pan.

3. Bake 23 to 25 minutes or until center is firm to the touch. Do not overbake. Sprinkle with remaining ⅓ cup semisweet chips and ⅓ cup white chips. Let stand until chips soften; spread chocolate over bars. Cool completely in pan on wire rack. *Makes 16 bars*

V

Very Berry Cheesecake Dump Cake, 47

W

Walnuts

Apple Cake, 111
Applesauce Cake, 131
Applesauce Fudge Bars, 257
Applesauce Spice Bread, 202
Applesauce Spice Cake, 74
Butter Brickle Cake, 130
Carrot Banana Cake, 10
Cha-Cha-Cha Cherry Cake, 11
Chocolate Chip Pumpkin Bread, 200
Cinnamon Apple Ring, 193
Cinnamon Wheat Brownies, 227
Classic Apple Dump Cake, 14
Cranberry Apple Dump Cake, 68
Cranberry Pear Cake, 72
Dark Chocolate Beer Bread, 195
Decadent Brownies, 240
Door County Bars, 247
Double Chocolate Walnut Bread, 198
Espresso Walnut Bars, 244
Favorite Potluck Carrot Cake, 133
Harvest Quick Bread, 210
Honey Brownies, 218
Lemony Banana Walnut Bread, 196
Mississippi Mud Bars, 273
No-Fuss Bar Cookies, 267
Nutty Chocolate Cherry Brownies, 239
Pistachio Walnut Bundt Cake, 143
Rocky Road Brownies, 235
Rocky Road Cake, 109

Walnuts *(continued)*

Simply Scrumptious Apple Cake, 95
Spiced Pumpkin Beer Bread, 207
Taste of the Tropics Cake, 90
Whole Wheat Date Nut Bread, 185
Winter Squash Cake, 73
Zucchini Spice Bundt Cake, 162

White Chocolate

Apricot Double Chip Dump Cake, 64
Cappuccino Crunch Bars, 254
Chocolate Cookie Magic Bars, 246
Cookies 'n' Cream Cake, 163
Double Chocolate Chip Snack Cake, 126
Light Chocolate Bundt Cake, 144
Mississippi Mud Bars, 273
Piña Colada Cookie Bars, 262
Raspberry Coconut Bars, 253
Red Velvet Cake, 60
White Chocolate Almond Brownies, 233
White Chocolate Chunk Brownies, 219
White Chocolate Cream Cheese Frosting, 215
Whole Wheat Brownies, 234
Whole Wheat Carrot Cake, 124
Whole Wheat Date Nut Bread, 185
Winter Squash Cake, 73

Z

Zucchini

Zucchini Orange Bread, 189
Zucchini Spice Bundt Cake, 162

Metric Conversion Chart

VOLUME MEASUREMENTS (dry)

⅛ teaspoon = 0.5 mL
¼ teaspoon = 1 mL
½ teaspoon = 2 mL
¾ teaspoon = 4 mL
1 teaspoon = 5 mL
1 tablespoon = 15 mL
2 tablespoons = 30 mL
¼ cup = 60 mL
⅓ cup = 75 mL
½ cup = 125 mL
⅔ cup = 150 mL
¾ cup = 175 mL
1 cup = 250 mL
2 cups = 1 pint = 500 mL
3 cups = 750 mL
4 cups = 1 quart = 1 L

VOLUME MEASUREMENTS (fluid)

1 fluid ounce (2 tablespoons) = 30 mL
4 fluid ounces (½ cup) = 125 mL
8 fluid ounces (1 cup) = 250 mL
12 fluid ounces (1½ cups) = 375 mL
16 fluid ounces (2 cups) = 500 mL

WEIGHTS (mass)

½ ounce = 15 g
1 ounce = 30 g
3 ounces = 90 g
4 ounces = 120 g
8 ounces = 225 g
10 ounces = 285 g
12 ounces = 360 g
16 ounces = 1 pound = 450 g

DIMENSIONS

¹/₁₆ inch = 2 mm
⅛ inch = 3 mm
¼ inch = 6 mm
½ inch = 1.5 cm
¾ inch = 2 cm
1 inch = 2.5 cm

OVEN TEMPERATURES

250°F = 120°C
275°F = 140°C
300°F = 150°C
325°F = 160°C
350°F = 180°C
375°F = 190°C
400°F = 200°C
425°F = 220°C
450°F = 230°C

BAKING PAN SIZES

Utensil	Size in Inches/Quarts	Metric Volume	Size in Centimeters
Baking or Cake Pan (square or rectangular)	8×8×2	2 L	20×20×5
	9×9×2	2.5 L	23×23×5
	12×8×2	3 L	30×20×5
	13×9×2	3.5 L	33×23×5
Loaf Pan	8×4×3	1.5 L	20×10×7
	9×5×3	2 L	23×13×7
Round Layer Cake Pan	8×1½	1.2 L	20×4
	9×1½	1.5 L	23×4
Pie Plate	8×1¼	750 mL	20×3
	9×1¼	1 L	23×3
Baking Dish or Casserole	1 quart	1 L	—
	1½ quart	1.5 L	—
	2 quart	2 L	—